I HAVE A
DREAM

I HAVE A DREAM

THE SPEECHES THAT CHANGED HISTORY

FERDIE ADDIS

Michael O'Mara Books Limited

First published in Great Britain in 2011 by
Michael O'Mara Books Limited
9 Lion Yard
Tremadoc Road
London SW4 7NQ

A CIP catalogue record for this book is available from the British Library.

Papers used by Michael O'Mara Books Limited are natural, recyclable products
made from wood grown in sustainable forests. The manufacturing processes
conform to the environmental regulations of the country of origin.

ISBN: 978-1-84317-586-5

2 3 4 5 6 7 8 9 10

www.mombooks.com

Cover design by Patrick Knowles

Designed and typeset by Envy Design Ltd

Printed and bound in Great Britain by Clays Ltd, St Ives plc

CONTENTS

INTRODUCTION

A truly brilliant speech is an extraordinary thing. The great lines resonate with amazing power. Sometimes the secret lies in the rhythm of the words: 'fourscore and seven years ago our fathers brought forth on this continent …' Sometimes the art comes from a powerful metaphor or image: 'I know I have the body but of a weak and feeble woman; but I have the heart and stomach of a king.' Sometimes a speech derives its impact from an ideal or a compelling vision: 'I have a dream that my four little children will one day live in a nation where they will not be judged by the colour of their skin, but by the content of their character.'

These lines have lived on in our collective memories. It's impossible to think about the Battle of Britain, for example, without hearing Churchill's gruff tones: 'we shall

fight on the beaches. We shall fight on the landing grounds
…' No one could forget in November 2008 the first black
US president telling the world 'change has come to
America.'

But can a speech, however memorable, change history?
It would be easy to think not. Looking at the great sweep
of civilization's story, the battles and revolutions, the
marches and migrations, the economic upheavals, it would
be easy to conclude that historical forces are much too vast
and powerful to be much affected by any single person,
much less a single speech. In centuries past, you might
argue, old-fashioned chroniclers, with their focus on
individuals, failed to see the wood for the trees.

But what if the opposite is true? To talk in terms of
'nations' and 'social forces', of 'entrenched cultural norms'
and 'demographic shifts' is to lose sight of the fact that
history is made not by abstractions but by people – people
with ambitions, feelings, desires and, above all, ideas. When
we ignore history's human dimension, we are failing to see
the trees for the wood.

And although words can't fight battles, or power
factories, they certainly can drive people. There are times
when people are in the grip of intense but inarticulate
feelings. At those times, the right speech can transform an
incoherent surge of emotion into a burst of positive,
directed activity. John Ball did this when he gave his
sermon at the Peasants' Revolt. Hitler also used this power
to achieve his own evil ends, channelling German
resentment of economic woes into a murderous hatred of
the Jews.

At other times, a speech can change the mood of a population – inspiring them with new courage or resolve. When Emmeline Pankhurst told women she was 'a soldier temporarily absent from the fields of battle', she gave them new heart in the struggle for women's suffrage. When Franklin Roosevelt told his country of the Japanese attack on Pearl Harbor – 'a date that will live in infamy' – he brought a newly resolute America into the Second World War.

And then there are times when a speech delivers an important message. Nehru announced the birth of India as a 'tryst with destiny'. Macmillan marked the end of imperialism when he talked about the 'wind of change'. When Malcolm X spoke of 'the ballot or the bullet', it was a warning to the enemies of Civil Rights.

This book is the story of these moments, when the words of a single man or woman really can change the world. Some of the speeches will be familiar, others less so. They were made by priests, popes, peasants, slaves, soldiers, dictators, prime ministers, presidents and Indian chiefs. They were delivered in all the different corners of the globe. But they all have something in common: in one way or another, these speeches really did make history.

8TH–1ST CENTURIES BC

THE CLASSICAL ORATORS

It was in Ancient Greece that the art of rhetoric first began to flourish. The cramped city-states of the Greek world made perfect stages for orators to display their skills. And where, as was the case in many cities, power was relatively fragmented, a persuasive speaker could wield considerable influence over small and easily swayed political assemblies.

In legal matters too, the best speakers had a distinct advantage. In democratic Athens, cases were tried by large citizen juries – who appreciated fine words as much as solid argument.

Indeed, one of literature's first heroes – Homer's Odysseus – was most admired not for his fighting skills but for his cunning way with words.

Like philosophy and science, rhetoric too was soon

codified. Itinerant teachers called 'sophists' gave lectures on the subject, and young Greek aristocrats flocked to their feet to learn the tricks of the trade. Aristotle, the tutor of Alexander the Great and one of Greece's foremost intellectuals, laid out the rules of style and argument in a monumental work – *The Art of Rhetoric*. Public speaking became the cornerstone of any proper education.

—— THE SPEECHES ——

HOMER – THE ILIAD

Homer's Iliad *is perhaps the first and greatest work in the whole of Western literature. It is also full of great speeches, of which the following is among the most famous. Agamemnon, high king of the Greeks, has insulted Achilles, the army's greatest fighter. In typically overblown style, Achilles gets up to reply:*

Wine-bibber … with the face of a dog and the heart of a hind, you never dare to go out with the host in fight, nor yet with our chosen men in ambuscade. You shun this as you do death itself.

… Therefore I say, and swear it with a great oath … that hereafter they [*the Greeks*] shall look fondly for Achilles and shall not find him. In the day of your distress, when your men fall dying by the murderous hand of Hector, you shall not know how to help them, and shall rend your heart with rage for the hour when you offered insult to the best of the Achaeans.

PERICLES – FUNERAL ORATION

Pericles was the greatest leader of Ancient Athens, the man who most of all was responsible for establishing the city as the home of art, culture and democracy. In this speech, which has since often been held up as a masterpiece of the rhetorical arts, he is commemorating those who had died in the first year of the Peloponnesian war against Sparta.

Such is the city for whose sake these men nobly fought and died; they could not bear the thought that she might be taken from them; and every one of us who survive should gladly toil on her behalf.

[. . .]

Such was the end of these men; they were worthy of Athens, and the living need not desire to have a more heroic spirit, although they may pray for a less fatal issue. The value of such a spirit is not to be expressed in words.

[. . .]

For the whole earth is the sepulchre of famous men; not only are they commemorated by columns and inscriptions in their own country, but in foreign lands there dwells also an unwritten memorial of them, graven not on stone but in the hearts of men. Make them your examples, and, esteeming courage to be freedom and freedom to be happiness, do not weigh too nicely the perils of war.

DEMOSTHENES – THIRD PHILIPPIC

Demosthenes was an Athenian statesman of the fourth century BC *who devoted his life to the art of public speaking. It is said that when he was young he used to train his voice by speaking with pebbles in his mouth, or shouting over the roar of the waves.*

His most famous speeches are the Philippics, *so called because they dealt with Philip II of Macedon, a northern king who, Demosthenes was convinced, posed a mortal threat to Athenian freedom and democracy.*

Despite Demosthenes' efforts, Athens fell to Philip's armies. But the Philippics *lived on as rhetorical models for generations to come.*

Many things could be named by the Olynthians today, which would have saved them from destruction if only they had then foreseen them. Many could be named by the Orites, many by the Phocians, many by every ruined city.

But of what use to them is that?

14

[. . .]

So we too, Athenians, as long as we are safe, blessed with a very great city, ample advantages, and the fairest repute—what are we to do? Perhaps some of my hearers have long been eager to ask that question. [. . .] To begin with ourselves, we must make provision for our defence, I mean with war-galleys, funds, and men; for even if all other states succumb to slavery, we surely must fight the battle of liberty.

CICERO – THIRTEENTH PHILIPPIC

Cicero was the finest orator Ancient Rome ever produced. As a young man, his prowess in the courts was legendary – and feared. His speeches could ruin careers and demolish reputations.

His skill soon carried him to the forefront of Roman politics, just as the civil wars were tearing the Republic apart. His Philippics, named after Demosthenes' orations, were a set of fourteen speeches he made attacking Mark Antony, leader of one of the most powerful factions. At the time this speech (the thirteenth) was made, Antony was asking the senate for peace. Cicero was determined that there should be war.

You have repealed the acts of Marcus Antonius; you have taken down his laws; you have voted that they were carried by violence, and with a disregard of the auspices; you have called out the levies throughout all Italy; you have pronounced that colleague and ally of all wickedness a public enemy. What peace can there be with this man? Even if he were a foreign enemy, still, after such actions as have taken place, it would be scarcely possible, by any means whatever, to have peace. Though seas and mountains, and vast regions lay between you, still you would hate such a man without seeing him. But these men will stick to your eyes, and when they can, to your very throats; for what fences will be strong enough for us to restrain savage beasts?

c. AD 26
THE SERMON ON THE MOUNT

JESUS OF NAZARETH
(*c.* 5 BC – *c.* AD 30)

No one really knows when Jesus gave the Sermon on the Mount. In fact, concrete facts about Jesus's life are hard to come by. All we know for sure is that there was a Jewish preacher by that name, who was crucified in Jerusalem sometime during the reign of the Roman Emperor Tiberius. Beyond that, the details of His life are uncertain.

None of which prevented Him from making perhaps the most influential speech of all time – at least, if it was a speech, and if He made it. There are those who argue that what the Gospels present as a single sermon was in fact a poetic running together of three years' worth of teachings.

But the facts of what happened are, perhaps, less important than the story of what was believed to have happened, as found in the Gospels that were written by Jesus's followers long after His death. These books, the central scriptures of Christianity, record a speech which, in the context of ancient religion, is truly revolutionary. Jesus took centuries of traditional Jewish law, handed down all the way from Moses, and stood them on their head.

—— THE SPEECH ——

[*The following version is taken from the Gospel of St Matthew*]

Blessed are the poor in spirit: for theirs is the kingdom of heaven.

Blessed are they that mourn: for they shall be comforted.

Blessed are the meek: for they shall inherit the earth.

Blessed are they which do hunger and thirst after righteousness: for they shall be filled.

Blessed are the merciful: for they shall obtain mercy.

Blessed are the pure in heart: for they shall see God.

Blessed are the peacemakers: for they shall be called the children of God.

Blessed are they which are persecuted for righteousness' sake: for theirs is the kingdom of heaven.

[. . .]

Ye have heard that it was said by them of old time, Thou shalt not kill; and whosoever shall kill shall be in danger of the judgement:

But I say unto you, that whosoever is angry with his brother without a cause shall be in danger of the judgement ...

Ye have heard that it was said by them of old time, Thou shalt not commit adultery:

But I say unto you, that whosoever looketh on a woman to lust after her hath committed adultery with her already in his heart ...

It hath been said, Whosoever shall put away his wife, let him give her a writing of divorcement:

But I say unto you, That whosoever shall put away his wife, saving for the cause of fornication, causeth her to commit adultery: and whosoever shall marry her that is divorced committeth adultery.

Again, ye have heard that it hath been said by them of

old time, Thou shalt not forswear thyself, but shalt perform unto the Lord thine oaths:

But I say unto you, Swear not at all; neither by heaven; for it is God's throne:

Nor by the earth; for it is his footstool: neither by Jerusalem; for it is the city of the great King …

Ye have heard that it hath been said, An eye for an eye, and a tooth for a tooth:

But I say unto you, That ye resist not evil: but whosoever shall smite thee on thy right cheek, turn to him the other also.

[…]

After this manner therefore pray ye:

Our Father which art in heaven, Hallowed be thy name.
Thy kingdom come. Thy will be done in earth, as it is in heaven.
Give us this day our daily bread.
And forgive us our debts, as we forgive our debtors.
And lead us not into temptation, but deliver us from evil:
For thine is the kingdom, and the power, and the glory, for ever. Amen.

I HAVE A DREAM

—— THE CONSEQUENCES ——

This speech sets out the foundation for a radical new system of religious belief. The old justice-based morality of 'an eye for an eye' is replaced by a completely different set of rules, valuing meek self-effacement over righteous indignation.

Spread by the four Evangelists, Mark, Matthew, Luke and John, the message of the Gospels (literally 'good news') proved powerful beyond imagining. Within 100 years of Jesus's death the Roman Emperor Nero was troubled by such large numbers of 'Christians' that he took to setting them on fire to light his gardens.

Some 200 years after that, another emperor, Constantine the Great, saw which way the wind was blowing and made Christianity the official religion of the whole Roman Empire, from the forests of Germany to the Sahara Desert.

A thousand years later, as the Christian states of Europe started expanding their own empires, the message of the Sermon was carried (sometimes at swordpoint) to the furthest corners of the globe. Today, in all its many forms, Christianity remains the most popular religion on the planet.

1096

THE COUNCIL OF CLERMONT

POPE URBAN II
(*c*.1035–1099)

By the end of the eleventh century, Western Europe
was beginning to haul itself out of the long slump
of the Dark Ages. But while the outlines of modern
nations were beginning to emerge in the West, in the East,
the light of civilization was on the wane. The Byzantine
Empire, devastated by centuries of Islamic invasion, had
been reduced to a tiny nub around its capital,
Constantinople.

Eventually, in 1095, Byzantium's Emperor, Alexius I
Comnenus, swallowed his pride and send word to Pope
Urban II in Rome asking for help against the marauding
infidels.

Despite long-standing religious differences between East
and West, Pope Urban was sympathetic to the plight of his
fellow Christians. Apart from the obvious religious motives,

a military mission to the East presented some rather more wordly benefits. Byzantium's lost empire was rich territory, a tempting bounty for land-starved western knights. And, by uniting them against a common enemy, Urban could hope to put an end to the constant petty feuding that still threatened to tear Europe apart.

So, in 1096, the Pope held a gathering of clerics and kings at Clermont in France. There, he made a speech that changed the course of the Middle Ages, and left an indelible mark on Western culture:

—— THE SPEECH ——

Oh, race of Franks, race from across the mountains, race chosen and beloved by God …! To you our discourse is addressed and for you our exhortation is intended.

[…]

From the confines of Jerusalem and the city of Constantinople a horrible tale has gone forth and very frequently has been brought to our ears, namely, that a race from the kingdom of the Persians, an accursed race, a race utterly alienated from God … has invaded the lands of those Christians and has depopulated them by the sword, pillage and fire …

They destroy the altars, after having defiled them with their uncleanness. They circumcize the Christians, and the blood of the circumcision they either spread upon the altars or pour into the vases of the baptismal font. When they wish to torture people by a base death, they perforate their navels, and dragging forth the extremity of the intestines, bind it to a stake; then with flogging they lead the victim around until, the viscera having gushed forth, the victim falls prostrate upon the ground.

[. . .]

The kingdom of the Greeks is now dismembered by them and deprived of territory so vast in extent that it cannot be traversed in a march of two months. On whom therefore is the labour of avenging these wrongs and of recovering this territory incumbent, if not upon you? You, upon whom above other nations God has conferred remarkable glory in arms, great courage, bodily activity, and strength to humble the hairy scalp of those who resist you.

Since this land which you inhabit, shut in on all sides by the seas and surrounded by the mountain peaks, is too narrow for your large population; nor does it abound in wealth; and it furnishes scarcely food enough for its cultivators. Hence it is that you murder one another, that you wage war, and that frequently you perish by mutual wounds.

Let therefore hatred depart from among you, let your

quarrels end, let wars cease, and let all dissensions and controversies slumber. Enter upon the road to the Holy Sepulchre [*an ancient church marking the burial place of Christ*]; wrest that land from the wicked race, and subject it to yourselves ... The land is fruitful above others, like another paradise of delights.

God has conferred upon you above all nations great glory in arms. Accordingly undertake this journey for the remission of your sins, with the assurance of the imperishable glory of the kingdom of heaven.

[. . .]

—— THE CONSEQUENCES ——

Urban had aimed his speech at kings and princes, but so powerful was his message (and so compelling his promise of 'remission of sins') that huge crowds of peasants trooped towards the Holy Land, armed with little more than pitchforks and blind faith. Of course, such armaments were little match for the disciplined Turkish archers who massacred them soon after they crossed into Asia.

But Europe's nobles had also obeyed the Pope's call. In 1099, a crusader army under the Count of Toulouse arrived at Jerusalem, which they then proceeded to sack and pillage in time-honoured Western fashion.

Once the bloodshed was over, the crusaders discovered a culture that was in many ways more advanced than their own. Christian traders brought back silks and spices from the East. Western Scholars translated Arabic texts, often themselves translations of forgotten works from Ancient Greece.

Jerusalem stayed in crusader hands for less than 100 years, but it was from this cultural exchange that we get, for instance, the concept of 'zero', and of 'algebra'. It was not Pope Urban's intention, but it was after his words at Clermont that the West began to open its eyes to the wider world.

1381
WHEN ADAM DELVED
AND EVE SPAN

JOHN BALL
(c.1338–1381)

Late-fourteenth-century England was a harsh and largely miserable place. Decades of war and plague had reduced the masses to constant poverty, and the ruling nobility kept great chunks of the population in a state of destitute serfdom, tied to the land and crippled by taxes.

Into this troubled world stepped John Ball, a travelling priest and full-time rabble-rouser who preached egalitarianism. Naturally he was soon excommunicated by the Church for promoting such seditious doctrine, and the King's Officers kept him under almost permanent arrest, but, in 1381, a popular uprising plucked him from obscurity (and the Royal Prison at Maidstone) and elevated him to the status of rebel legend.

The uprising was the Peasants' Revolt, a chaotic movement of peasant farmers protesting against the so-called Third Poll Tax. Led by the enigmatic Wat Tyler, bands of pitchfork-waving peasants from Essex and Kent converged on London, meeting just south of the city at Blackheath.

This was John Ball's moment. Facing the angry mob, he prepared to deliver a speech that would go down in history.

—— THE SPEECH ——

When Adam delved and Eve span, who was then the gentleman?

From the beginning all men by nature were created alike, and our bondage or servitude came in by the unjust oppression of naughty men. For if God would have had any bondmen from the beginning, he would have appointed who should be bond, and who free.

And therefore I exhort you to consider that now the time is come, appointed to us by God, in which ye may (if ye will) cast off the yoke of bondage, and recover liberty.

—— THE CONSEQUENCES ——

Fired up by John Ball's sermon, the rebels poured into London where they terrified the city-folk and caused havoc in the town, torching the palace of the aristocrat John of Gaunt and murdering Simon Sudbury, the Archbishop of Canterbury.

Finally, the King himself rode out to talk to the rebels. It looked like victory was in their grasp – but, during the parlay, the rebel leader Wat Tyler was struck down by the Lord Mayor of London. It was said that the Lord Mayor objected to the uncouth way in which Tyler drank his beer.

The King promised concessions, and the rebels grudgingly returned home. But as soon as they had dispersed, the concessions were abandoned and the rebel leaders arrested. On 12 July 1381, John Ball was hanged, drawn and quartered.

His revolt had ended in failure, but his legacy proved more enduring. Over the following century, the institution of serfdom in Britain slowly lost ground. Meanwhile, Ball's radical and anticlerical form of Christianity spread, finally emerging in the English Reformation.

It was from this Protestant tradition that, 400 years after John Ball's speech, America's Founding Fathers drew their inspiration. When they declared 'that all men are created equal', they also, unconsciously, echoed his words.

1588
ELIZABETH REVIEWS
THE ARMY AT TILBURY

ELIZABETH I

(1533–1603)

In 1588, England faced one of the greatest threats in the country's history. Philip II of Spain had dispatched a huge 'Armada' of ships towards the coast of Flanders. There, just across the English Channel, the allied Duke of Parma stood waiting with a vast army to invade the British Isles. If Parma could meet the Armada, and use it to land on England's shore, the outnumbered defenders would stand little chance.

The small English army mustered at Tilbury on the Thames Estuary, where it was thought the Duke of Parma would try to make his landing. There they waited, as the Armada, sighted off Cornwall on 19 July, continued its inexorable advance.

It was under these dire circumstances that Elizabeth herself arrived to see the troops. Eyewitness accounts are few and unreliable, but the tradition is that she appeared not in court dress but wearing a kingly breastplate and brandishing a silver truncheon. Although her exact words were not recorded at the time, a letter from 1623 gives this version of her speech.

—— THE SPEECH ——

We have been persuaded by some that are careful of our safety, to take heed how we commit our selves to armed multitudes, for fear of treachery; but I assure you I do not desire to live to distrust my faithful and loving people.

Let tyrants fear. I have always so behaved myself that, under God, I have placed my chiefest strength and safeguard in the loyal hearts and good-will of my subjects; and therefore I am come amongst you, as you see, at this time, not for my recreation and disport, but being resolved, in the midst and heat of the battle, to live and die amongst you all; to lay down for my God, and for my kingdom, and my people, my honour and my blood, even in the dust.

I know I have the body but of a weak and feeble woman; but I have the heart and stomach of a king, and of a king of England too, and think foul scorn that Parma or Spain, or any prince of Europe, should dare to invade the borders of my realm; to which rather than any dishonour shall grow by me, I myself will take up arms, I myself will be your general, judge, and rewarder of every one of your virtues in the field. I know already, for your forwardness you have deserved rewards and crowns; and We do assure you in the word of a prince, they shall be duly paid you. In the mean time, my lieutenant general [*the Earl of Leicester*] shall be in my stead, than whom never prince commanded a more noble or worthy subject; not doubting but by your obedience to my general, by your concord in the camp, and your valour in the field, we shall shortly have a famous victory over those enemies of my God, of my kingdom, and of my people.

— THE CONSEQUENCES —

Elizabeth was not to know that in fact the danger had already passed. While she was delivering her brave oration, the Armada was rounding the tip of Scotland, having been hotly pursued most of the way by the victorious British fleet.

The Duke of Parma still lurked menacingly across the Channel, but the Spanish fleet was never going to manage to pick him up as they had promised. As summer gave way to autumn, the battle-scarred ships struggled through the North Atlantic, where unseasonable storms drove many to destruction on the rocky Scottish and Irish coasts. Philip's invincible Armada was humiliated and ruined.

Although Elizabeth never got to prove her manly mettle in a fight, it didn't take long for poetic tributes to appear. The 'Virgin Queen' and her appearance at Tilbury became the stuff of legend. Elizabeth, with the help of her propagandists, was transformed into a symbol, an idealized vision of the spirit of England itself.

1653

DISMISSING THE RUMP PARLIAMENT

OLIVER CROMWELL
(1599–1658)

Oliver Cromwell first came to prominence as a successful commander in the Parliamentarian army, fighting with the 'roundheads' against King Charles I's 'cavaliers' in the English Civil War. From 1642 to 1648, battles raged up and down Britain until at last the royalists were defeated.

In 1649, after long but unsuccessful negotiations, the stubborn king was executed by order of Parliament. Cromwell was by now the most powerful man in the country.

His aim was then to establish a government of 'saints' – pious men drawn from his own Congregationalist faith – but to do that constitutionally he needed the change to come from the so-called 'Rump Parliament' of MPs who had stayed on after Charles's death.

For years, Cromwell waited for his glorious reformation. But as time went by, it became clear that the Rump's MPs were only interested in their own well-being.

Finally, in 1653, he could wait no longer. Accompanied by a group of soldiers, he appeared in the House of Commons and made the following blistering speech.

—— THE SPEECH ——

It is high time for me to put an end to your sitting in this place, which you have dishonoured by your contempt of all virtue, and defiled by your practice of every vice.

Ye are a factious crew, and enemies to all good government. Ye are a pack of mercenary wretches, and would like Esau sell your country for a mess of pottage, and like Judas betray your God for a few pieces of money.

Is there a single virtue now remaining amongst you? Is there one vice you do not possess?

Ye have no more religion than my horse. Gold is your God. Which of you have not bartered your conscience for bribes? Is there a man amongst you that has the least care for the good of the Commonwealth?

Ye sordid prostitutes have you not defiled this sacred place, and turned the Lord's temple into a den of thieves, by your immoral principles and wicked practices?

Ye are grown intolerably odious to the whole nation. You were deputed here by the people to get grievances redressed, are yourselves become the greatest grievance.

Your country therefore calls upon me to cleanse this Augean stable, by putting a final period to your iniquitous proceedings in this House; and which by God's help, and the strength he has given me, I am now come to do.

I command ye therefore, upon the peril of your lives, to depart immediately out of this place.

Go, get you out! Make haste! Ye venal slaves be gone! So! Take away that shining bauble there, [*indicating the ceremonial mace of office*] and lock up the doors.

In the name of God, go!

—— THE CONSEQUENCES ——

Even by seventeenth-century standards this was an extraordinary piece of invective, delivered with the white-hot anger of an Old Testament prophet. This was Cromwell as God's messenger, sweeping away the corruption of the old parliamentary order.

After the dissolution of the Rump Parliament, the running of the state was taken up by the council of senior army officers, who, at last, established the long-hoped-for Parliament of 'Saints'. But, to Cromwell's dismay, this pious group of Protestant MPs proved no better than the last parliament. He had asked them to devise a programme of reforms that would make England a truly godly country, but in December 1653, exhausted by petty squabbles, the Saints gave up, and voted their own assembly out of existence.

Forced to admit that his experiment had failed, Cromwell took matters into his own hands, appointing himself Lord Protector in 1654. As head of state, he had taken the place of the king he had worked so hard to depose. Despite all his efforts, when Cromwell died in 1658, he left behind no political system that could survive him, and, two years after his death, the country reverted to the old monarchy under King Charles II. That monarchy has remained intact to this day.

1794

THE POLITICAL
PHILOSOPHY OF
TERROR

MAXIMILIEN ROBESPIERRE
(1758–1794)

Robespierre was arguably the finest orator of the French Revolution. His background was in law – and as a young man he had campaigned to abolish the death penalty. However his career took a change into politics and in the months before the French Revolution he became the leader of the radical Jacobin Club, which demanded exile or execution of the king and queen.

The mobs of Paris stormed the Tuileries Palace in 1792 and the Jacobins seized power. As leader of the Committee for Public Safety, Robespierre became the most powerful man in France. Faced with the threat of counter-revolution following the execution of Louis XVI, he masterminded a ruthless suppression of all opposition: perhaps the corrupting influence of power had changed his view on the sanctity of life. By July 1794, 2,400 people had been executed at the Guillotine, and countless more on the street in Robespierre's Reign of Terror.

In February 1794, Robespierre addressed the National Convention, defending his brutal methods for enforcing justice. The speech, though long (onlookers claimed he was on his feet for three hours), was eloquent, rousing and chilling; the end absolutely justifies the means.

—— THE SPEECH ——

[. . .]

But, to found and consolidate democracy, to achieve the peaceable reign of the constitutional laws, we must end the war of liberty against tyranny and pass safely across the storms of the revolution: such is the aim of the revolutionary system that you have enacted. Your conduct, then, ought also to be regulated by the stormy circumstances in which the republic is placed; and the plan of your administration must result from the spirit of the revolutionary government combined with the general principles of democracy.

Now, what is the fundamental principle of the democratic or popular government – that is, the essential spring which makes it move? It is virtue; I am speaking of the public virtue which effected so many prodigies in Greece and Rome and which ought to produce much more surprising ones in republican France; of that virtue which is nothing other than the love of country and of its laws.

But as the essence of the republic or of democracy is equality, it follows that the love of country necessarily includes the love of equality.

[. . .]

If the spring of popular government in time of peace is virtue, the springs of popular government in revolution are at once virtue and terror: virtue, without which terror is fatal; terror, without which virtue is powerless. Terror is nothing other than justice, prompt, severe, inflexible; it is therefore an emanation of virtue; it is not so much a special principle as it is a consequence of the general principle of democracy applied to our country's most urgent needs.

It has been said that terror is the principle of despotic government. Does your government therefore resemble despotism? Yes, as the sword that gleams in the hands of the heroes of liberty resembles that with which the henchmen of tyranny are armed. Let the despot govern by terror his brutalized subjects; he is right, as a despot. Subdue by terror the enemies of liberty, and you will be right, as founders of the Republic. The government of the revolution is liberty's despotism against tyranny. Is force made only to protect crime? And is the thunderbolt not destined to strike the heads of the proud?

[. . .]

—— THE CONSEQUENCES ——

This address to the Convention served as a warning, in effect, of worse to come. The Terror reached its apogee in the months that followed. Robespierre's political enemies formed a conspiracy against him. When a decree for his arrest was passed, Robespierre fled and the National Convention, of which he was elected president, declared him an outlaw. On 28 July 1794, he and nineteen others were sent to the Guillotine. This was, incidentally, the only execution he ever witnessed. Eighty more of his followers suffered the same fate the next day.

In the struggle to enforce his concept of virtue, Robespierre's fanaticism became a threat to his own ideals. His death marked the beginning of the defeat of the Revolution. Power moved from the radicals to the conservatives, the Jacobin Clubs were closed down and freedom of worship was restored in February 1795.

1814
FAREWELL TO
THE OLD GUARD

NAPOLEON BONAPARTE
(1769–1821)

Napoleon Bonaparte was born into a family of modest rank. At military school they called him 'the little corporal' because he was so short. And, though he would rule France, he was a native of Corsica, and never lost his heavy Italian accent.

But nothing creates unlikely success stories like a revolution. In the years of chaos after the fall of the French monarchy in 1789, Napoleon rose swiftly through the ranks of the revolutionary army; in 1799, a bloodless coup made him first Consul and in 1804 Emperor of France.

The country was surrounded by hostile powers, but Napoleon was a superb general, and smashed the ailing states of Austria and Prussia to create an empire that stretched from Portugal to the Baltic Sea. His 'Grande Armée' was half a million strong.

His power was not to last. In 1812, he took 400,000 men east towards Moscow. Six months later, devastated by the Russian winter, the frostbitten survivors of the Grande Armée came limping painfully back.

By 1814, Napoleon was utterly defeated. The only soldiers that remained to him were the men of the Old Guard, an elite of veteran troops, utterly devoted to their Emperor. Abandoned by his generals, encircled by enemy armies, Napoleon gathered the men and delivered the following speech.

—— THE SPEECH ——

Soldiers of my Old Guard:
I bid you farewell.

For twenty years I have constantly accompanied you on the road to honour and glory. In these latter times, as in the days of our prosperity, you have invariably been models of courage and fidelity.

With men such as you our cause could not be lost; but the war would have been interminable; it would have been civil war, and that would have entailed deeper misfortunes on France.

I have sacrificed all of my interests to those of the country.

I HAVE A DREAM

I go, but you, my friends, will continue to serve France. Her happiness was my only thought. It will still be the object of my wishes.

Do not regret my fate; if I have consented to survive, it is to serve your glory. I intend to write the history of the great achievements we have performed together.

Adieu, my friends.

Would I could press you all to my heart.

—— THE CONSEQUENCES ——

With only 8,000 soldiers remaining against the combined armies of Europe, Napoleon was jumping before he could be pushed. But the Guardsmen appear to have bought his story. Some of them wept openly as Napoleon embraced their leader, General Petit, and cradled their eagle standard in his arms.

After this final farewell, Napoleon abdicated. He was exiled to Elba, in the Mediterranean, to rule as 'Emperor' over the island's population of peasants and goatherds.

But it soon became apparent that Napoleon intended to do more than just sit around writing history books. Less than a year later, he had escaped back to France, had raised another army, and was marching north to war.

Sent to meet him was the Duke of Wellington, England's

finest general. On 18 June 1815, the armies clashed at the Battle of Waterloo. All day, Napoleon threw his troops fruitlessly at the British line. Finally, in desperation, he ordered the Guard to advance.

But that day, for the first and last time, their strength failed him. Decimated by volley fire, facing British bayonets, and caught in the flank by a brilliantly timed charge of light infantry, the Guard broke and retreated – and as word of the Guard's retreat spread, the whole French army broke and ran. Napoleon was exiled again, this time to St Helena, deep in the Atlantic, where he died in 1821.

Other Notable Lines

The motto of the Republic of France, *Liberté, Égalité, Fraternité*, has its origins in the heady atmosphere of the eighteenth century, when the philosopher-tyrants of the French Revolution were building the principles for a new kind of state. It was one of a series of slogans. *Unité* once had a chance at joining the great triumvirate. So did *Raison* and *Sûreté*.

But over the course of the 1790s, it was the familiar three that became pre-eminent. What's less well known is that in its earliest incarnations, the motto had a fourth, more bloodthirsty, part. As it appears on the oldest revolutionary placards, it reads: *Liberté, Égalité, Fraternité, ou la Mort* – Liberty, Equality, Fraternity, or Death!

1851
AR'N'T I A WOMAN?

SOJOURNER TRUTH
(*c*. 1 7 9 9 – 1 8 8 3)

Sojourner Truth was born into slavery in New York State around the turn of the nineteenth century. Known simply as Isabella, she served many owners before she was freed in 1827.

Along with her new-found freedom, Isabella found God, changed her name, and became a member of a succession of Methodist churches and unconventional religious movements, one of which preached that 1843 would mark the end of the world.

But as 1844 approached, and the apocalypse failed to materialize, Sojourner Truth began to concern herself with more worldly problems, especially emancipation and women's rights. After a few small-town appearances, she addressed a convention of feminists in Akron, Ohio. With this speech, she would step onto history's grand stage.

The audience had been browbeaten by a string of male preachers using selective quotations from the Bible to put rebellious women in their place. Then, amid gasps of racist outrage, the tall, dark figure of Sojourner Truth slowly approached the speaker's platform.

Records of what she said are inconsistent, but the best-known account was written twelve years later by the feminist Frances Gage, who had presided at the meeting. It was her story that made Sojourner Truth a legend.

—— THE SPEECH ——

The tumult subsided at once, and every eye was fixed on this almost Amazon form … At her first word there was a profound hush. She spoke in deep tones, which, though not loud, reached every ear in the house …

'Wall, chilern, whar dar is so much racket dar must be somethin' out o' kilter. I tink dat 'twixt de nigger of de Souf and de womin at de Norf, all talkin' 'bout rights, de white men will be in a fix pretty soon. But what's all dis here talkin' 'bout?

'Dat man ober dar say dat womin needs to be helped into carriages, and lifted ober ditches, and to hab de best place everywhar. Nobody eber halps me into carriages, or ober mudpuddles, or gibs me any best place!

[. . .]

'And ar'n't I a woman? Look at me! Look at my arm! … I have ploughed, and planted, and gathered into barns, and no man could head me! And ar'n't I a woman? I could work as much and eat as much as a man – when I could get it – and bear de lash as well! And ar'n't' I a woman? I have borne thirteen chilern, and seen 'em mos' all sold off the slavery, and when I cried out with my mother's grief, none but Jesus heard me! And ar'n't I a woman?

[. . .]

'Den dat little man in black dar, [*indicating a priest*] he say women can't have as much rights as men, 'cause Christ wan't a woman! Whar did your Christ come from?'

Rolling thunder couldn't have stilled that crowd as did those deep, wonderful tones, as she stood there with outstretched arms and eyes of fire. Raising her voice still louder, she repeated, 'Whar did your Christ come from? From God and a woman! Man had nothin' to do wid Him.'

—— THE CONSEQUENCES ——

According to Gage, Truth left her audience with 'streaming eyes, and hearts beating with gratitude'. But Gage's account of the speech is worryingly untrustworthy. She gives Truth a cod southern dialect, although the speaker was from the North. She invents thirteen children for her, when she only had five. And when she admires Truth's 'tremendous muscular power', she could be appraising a fine horse, not an intelligent and independent woman.

Harriet Beecher Stowe, celebrated author of the abolitionist novel *Uncle Tom's Cabin*, was another admirer of Truth. The two only met once, but the white author described her as 'mighty and dark as the gigantic depths of tropical forests', and commended her 'wonderful physical vigour'.

Sojourner Truth had become a myth, her true character buried beneath the stereotypes of her admirers. But although the myth was false – and demeaning – its impact was nonetheless deeply important. In 1863, Abraham Lincoln signed the Emancipation Proclamation. Slavery in the United States was finally over.

1863
THE GETTYSBURG
ADDRESS

PRESIDENT ABRAHAM LINCOLN
(1809–1865)

Abraham Lincoln, sixteenth president of the United States, came from humble stock. He grew up in a crude three-sided shack in Pigeon Creek, Indiana and served as a store clerk and postmaster, before finally finding his true calling in politics.

Lincoln arrived in Congress in 1847 to find a body politic that was tearing itself apart. The crucial question was slavery, to which Lincoln was naturally opposed. The keeping of slaves, he wrote, 'deprives our republican example of its just influence in the world – enables the enemies of free institutions, with plausibility, to taunt us as hypocrites … Our republican robe is soiled, and trailed in the dust.'

In 1860, Lincoln was elected president, which further alienated politicians from the slave-owning South. That year, the southern states formally seceded from the Union and in 1861, this new Confederacy took up arms against their northern neighbours.

The Civil War ebbed and flowed across the continent, as huge armies ground each other down with the new and terrible weapons of the industrial age. One of the bloodiest encounters was at Gettysburg in July 1863, where a northern army halted a southern advance, but at a terrible cost in lives.

So, it was amid a mood of doubt and despondency that Abraham Lincoln travelled to the battlefield to give a short speech commemorating the fallen.

—— THE SPEECH ——

Fourscore and seven years ago our fathers brought forth on this continent a new nation, conceived in liberty and dedicated to the proposition that all men are created equal.

Now we are engaged in a great civil war, testing whether that nation or any nation so conceived and so dedicated can long endure. We are met on a great battlefield of that war. We have come to dedicate a portion of that field as a final resting-place for those who here gave their lives that that nation might live. It is altogether fitting and proper that we should do this.

But, in a larger sense, we cannot dedicate, we cannot consecrate, we cannot hallow this ground. The brave men, living and dead who struggled here have consecrated it far above our poor power to add or detract. The world will little note nor long remember what we say here, but it can never forget what they did here.

It is for us the living rather to be dedicated here to the unfinished work which they who fought here have thus far so nobly advanced. It is rather for us to be here dedicated to the great task remaining before us – that from these honoured dead we take increased devotion to that cause for which they gave the last full measure of devotion – that we here highly resolve that these dead shall not have died in vain, that this nation under God shall have a new birth of freedom, and that government of the people, by the people, for the people shall not perish from the earth.

—— THE CONSEQUENCES ——

According to popular legend, Lincoln wrote this speech while on the train from Washington DC. He wasn't even the main speaker. The townsfolk of Gettysburg had already engaged Edward Everett, a celebrated orator, to deliver the main address – a two-hour eulogy that was, by all accounts, rated a great success.

Lincoln, it is recorded, thought his speech had been a

failure, and he was not alone. A reporter from *The Times* remarked: 'the ceremony was rendered ludicrous by some of the luckless sallies of that poor President Lincoln'.

But Lincoln and the reporter were both wrong. The Gettysburg Address is a rhetorical masterpiece, and is now one of the most quoted speeches in history, often considered alongside the constitution as a defining document of the United States.

To be so remembered is no more than Lincoln deserves. He was determined to see the war through to victory, and at last, victory did come, ensuring that government 'of the people, by the people, for the people' would survive the stern moral test that slavery and civil war had presented. Without Lincoln, America would be a different and lesser place today.

Sadly, Lincoln was not allowed much time to enjoy his victory. On 15 April 1865, he was shot by a Confederate sympathizer, and died shortly after.

Other Notable Lines

No sentence in history has had such an impact on the modern world as the one that was agreed by the Continental Congress of American States on 4 July 1776 as they declared their independence from Britain.

It was Thomas Jefferson who was most responsible for crafting the words that would create America. They were read in towns and villages across the new nation, and their echoes can still be heard today, defining the nature of what is now the most powerful country on earth.

The most famous sentence, one of the most well-known phrases in the English language, comes at the beginning – a bold and truly revolutionary statement of values:

We hold these truths to be self-evident, that all men are created equal, that they are endowed by their Creator with certain unalienable Rights, that among these are Life, Liberty and the pursuit of Happiness.

1877
I WILL FIGHT NO MORE FOREVER

CHIEF JOSEPH
(c. 1840–1904)

By the 1870s, America's Indian Wars were reaching their final act. In the South, Apache war bands were mounting a fitful resistance; on the Great Plains, the Sioux were holding out; but, by and large, the battle for the Wild West was over.

In the Wallowa Valley, Oregon, the Nez Percé tribe had suffered years of abuse from white settlers encroaching on their land. Their leader, Chief Joseph, knowing the might of the US Army, argued desperately for peace. But in 1877 a band of Indian warriors lost patience and killed some white settlers near the Salmon River.

US retaliation was not long coming, but the Nez Percé, with astonishing bravery, defeated the first detachment sent against them. Slowed down by women, children and the wounded, Joseph and his tribe began a fighting retreat towards the wilds of the Pacific North-West.

Finally, after travelling 1,170 miles across difficult country, they were intercepted by US cavalry at Bear Paw Mountain in Montana, just forty miles from the safety of the Canadian border.

Joseph's warriors were cold, weakened and out-numbered. So instead of fighting, the great chief did something that perhaps was braver. Meeting with the American officers, he made the following speech.

—— THE SPEECH ——

Tell General Howard [*the American commander*] I know his heart. What he told me before, I have it in my heart. I am tired of fighting. Our chiefs are killed; Looking Glass is dead, Too–hul–hul–sote is dead. The old men are all dead. It is the young men who say yes or no. He who led on the young men is dead.

It is cold, and we have no blankets; the little children are freezing to death. My people, some of them, have run away to the hills, and have no blankets, no food. No one knows where they are – perhaps freezing to death. I want to have time to look for my children, and see how many of them I can find. Maybe I shall find them among the dead.

Hear me, my chiefs! I am tired; my heart is sick and sad. From where the sun now stands, I will fight no more forever.

I HAVE A DREAM

—— THE CONSEQUENCES ——

Chief Joseph never returned to his ancestral home. For years, the Nez Percé were shuttled across America, from one reservation to another, while disease and despair corroded their old way of life. Joseph campaigned tirelessly to be allowed to return to the Wallowa Valley but despite the widespread sympathy that he earned, his request was never granted. In 1904 he died, according to his doctor, of a 'broken heart'.

But Joseph's great speech of surrender had a life of its own. It is probably the most quoted speech of any recorded by an American Indian, and no wonder. It is sad, short, simple, but at the same time an extraordinarily poetic testament to the suffering of a people. His final words, 'I will fight no more forever' echoed on in national consciousness and Joseph himself became a powerful symbol of the American Indian tragedy.

Even the name, Joseph, tells a story of the cultural vandalism that his people had suffered. His Indian title, which those two alien syllables replaced, was Hin-mut-too-uah-lat-kekht – Thunder Rolling in the Mountains.

Other Notable Lines

Captain Lawrence 'Titus' Oates was a member of Robert Scott's ill-fated expedition to the South Pole. They arrived at earth's southernmost tip on 17 January 1912, but discovered to their horror that a rival party, led by the Norwegian Roald Amundsen, had beaten them to it.

Despondent, the five explorers set off back to safety but Oates, frostbitten and limping, was slowing them down. On the evening of 16 March, he decided to sacrifice himself for the good of the party. As he left the tent, walking bootless into a howling blizzard, he announced with typical British understatement: 'I am just going outside – and may be some time.' His sacrifice was in vain, for Scott and his companions all perished within a few miles of safety.

1913
FREEDOM OR DEATH

EMMELINE PANKHURST
(1858–1928)

L iterate from an early age, Emmeline Pankhurst was bright, focused and politically aware. Certainly she was aware enough to realize very young that her life was to be circumscribed by an entrenched injustice. As a woman in Victorian England, her allotted destiny was to become a decorous helpmeet for some unappreciative man.

Barely out of her teens, Pankhurst started campaigning for female suffrage, and in 1903, she founded the organization that would make her famous, the Women's Social and Political Union, or WSPU. At first, these 'suffragettes' campaigned peacefully, but in 1908, tired of not being heard in the masculine confines of Westminster, the WSPU began a more militant programme.

That February, Emmeline served a month in prison for leading a deputation to the House of Commons. In 1909,

WSPU members began hunger strikes and were force-fed. By 1913, they had started smashing shop windows, vandalizing artworks and setting fires. Emmeline even helped explode a bomb outside the house of the Chancellor of the Exchequer, David Lloyd-George.

She was arrested and sentenced to three years, but was temporarily released after a string of hunger strikes. She took advantage of this brief moment of freedom to travel to America, where she made the following speech.

—— THE SPEECH ——

[. . .]

I am here as a soldier who has temporarily left the field of battle in order to explain … what civil war is like when civil war is waged by women …

I am here as a person who, according to the law courts of my country … is of no value to the community at all; and I am adjudged because of my life to be a dangerous person, under sentence of penal servitude in a convict prison.

[. . .]

Your forefathers decided that they must have representation for taxation, many, many years ago. When they felt they couldn't wait any longer, …

when every other means had failed, they began by the tea party at Boston, and they went on until they had won the independence of the United States of America.

[. . .]

When you have warfare things happen; people suffer; the non-combatants suffer as well as the combatants. And so it happens in civil war. When your forefathers threw the tea into Boston Harbour, a good many women had to go without their tea …

[. . .]

Now, I want to say to you who think women cannot succeed, we have brought the government of England to this position, that it has to face this alternative: either women are to be killed or women are to have the vote. I ask American men in this meeting, what would you say if in your state you were faced with that alternative, that you must either kill them or give them their citizenship? Well, there is only one answer to that alternative, there is only one way out - you must give those women the vote.

… That is the way in which we women of England are doing. Human life for us is sacred, but we say if any life is to be sacrificed it shall be ours; we won't do it ourselves, but we will put the enemy in the position where they will have to choose between giving us freedom or giving us death.

[. . .]

——THE CONSEQUENCES——

Emmeline's case was brilliantly calibrated to win over her American audience with her references to soldiers and civil war, and her paraphrasing of the American Revolutionary John Henry, who famously declared: 'give me liberty, or give me death!'

But Pankhurst's real genius was to realize that the key was to be heard at all. Although her methods might have been extreme, they worked, and the suffragette argument proved too powerful to be fought back for long. In February 1918, Parliament announced that all women over thirty would henceforth have the vote. In 1928, a new bill was set to give that right to all women over twenty-one. That year, a month before the bill was passed, Emmeline Pankhurst died, at the age of sixty-nine.

1915
IRELAND UNFREE

PATRICK PEARSE
(1879–1916)

By the beginning of the twentieth century, Ireland had been under British control on and off for more than five hundred years. In 1800, after a rebellion in 1798, the Act of Union had made the country part of the United Kingdom, ruled by the British Parliament in London.

Not that Ireland had quietly accepted its fate. Rebellions in 1803, 1848 and 1867, succeeding the 'Great Rebellion' of 1798, had been unsuccessful, but Irish nationalism had lived on, smouldering in the shadows.

Into this tinderbox nation was born Patrick Pearse, a Dublin schoolteacher who initially saw cultural renewal as the route to freedom. However, as the years went by, he started to support a bloodier kind of revolution. In 1913, he joined the newly established Irish Volunteer Force, and soon became involved in plans for a genuine armed uprising.

In 1915, Pearse gave a speech at the graveside of a recently deceased rebel called Jeremiah O'Donovan Rossa. Before making the speech, he asked a fellow nationalist how freely he should give rein to his more incendiary ideas. 'Make it hot as hell,' came the reply. 'Throw discretion to the winds.'

—— THE SPEECH——

[...]

We stand at Rossa's grave not in sadness but rather in exaltation of spirit that it has been given to us to come thus into so close a communion with that brave and splendid Gael. Splendid and holy causes are served by men who are themselves splendid and holy. O'Donovan Rossa was splendid in the proud manhood of him, splendid in the heroic grace of him, splendid in the Gaelic strength and clarity and truth of him. And all that splendour and pride and strength was compatible with a humility and a simplicity of devotion to Ireland, to all that was olden and beautiful and Gaelic in Ireland ... The clear true eyes of this man almost alone in his day envisioned Ireland as we of today would surely have her: not free merely, but Gaelic as well; not Gaelic merely, but free as well.

In a closer spiritual communion with him now than ever before, or perhaps ever again, in a spiritual communion with those of his day, living and dead, who suffered with him in English prisons, in communion of spirit too with our own dear comrades who suffer in English prisons today, and speaking on their behalf as well as our own, we pledge to Ireland our love, and we pledge to English rule in Ireland our hate.

[. . .]

The defenders of this Realm have worked well in secret and in the open. They think that they have pacified Ireland. They think that they have purchased half of us and intimidated the other half.

They think that they have foreseen everything, think that they have provided against everything, but the fools, the fools, the fools!

They have left us with our Fenian dead, and while Ireland holds these graves, Ireland unfree shall never be at peace.

—— THE CONSEQUENCES ——

On Easter Monday, 1916, Irish revolutionaries rose up against British occupying forces. From his headquarters in the Dublin General Post Office, Pearse read a declaration of independence for a new Irish Republic. Irish flags fluttered proudly over the city.

But the rebels were few and ill-equipped, no match for

the trained soldiers of the British garrison. After seven days of battle, Pearse ordered an unconditional surrender, to avoid further civilian casualties.

Before the rising, Pearse had written: 'the old heart of the earth needed to be warmed with the red wine of the battlefields. Such august homage was never offered to God as this, the homage of lives given gladly for love of country.'

But confronted with the harsh reality of street fighting, he lost his appetite for war. Not that the earth was to be deprived of her 'blood sacrifice.' At 3.30 a.m., on 3 May, Patrick Pearse was executed by firing squad.

The rising Pearse had helped create was met by ambivalence at the time. Many Irish regarded it as counter-productive – or worse. But in the manner of his death, and through his speeches and writings, Pearse became a martyr for the cause of armed Irish nationalism.

Other Notable Lines

No record was kept of the speech that made Patrick Henry a revolutionary legend. We have to rely on the testimony of a later historian, who put together an account based on the memories of eyewitnesses. The story is that in 1775 Patrick Henry was addressing the Virginia Convention, urging the necessity of revolting against English rule.

His grandstanding conclusion has passed into American mythology as the defining cry of the War of Independence:

'Our brethren are already in the field! Why stand we here idle? ... Is life so dear, or peace so sweet, as to be purchased at the price of chains and slavery? Forbid it, Almighty God! I know not what course others may take; but as for me, give me liberty or give me death!'

1916
Speech from the Dock

SIR ROGER CASEMENT
(1864–1916)

O f all the great Irish revolutionaries who played a part in 1916's Easter Rising against British rule, none is more colourful or controversial than Roger Casement.

His early life was spent in Africa, working for the British colonial service, but a stay in his native Ireland in 1904–6 made Casement a firm believer in Irish nationalism. In 1913, he renounced his Foreign Office post and committed full time to the cause.

In July 1914, Casement arranged a successful operation to smuggle guns to Ireland, providing much of the firepower that was later to be used in the Easter Rising. In October that year, soon after the outbreak of the First World War, he travelled to Berlin where he hoped to find German support for an armed revolution.

But by 1916, it had become clear that little German aid would be forthcoming. Disillusioned, he travelled back to Ireland by submarine to try to stop what he now saw as a doomed rebellion.

Even in this he was unsuccessful. Casement was captured soon after he put ashore. The Easter Rising took place without him and was swiftly and bloodily crushed. After a short trial that June, Casement was declared guilty of treason and made his final impassioned speech from the dock.

—— THE SPEECH ——

… There is an objection possibly not good in law but surely good on moral grounds against the application to me here of this English statute, 565 years old, that seeks to deprive an Irishman to-day of life and honour, not for 'adhering to the King's enemies' but for adhering to his own people.

Loyalty is a sentiment, not a law. It rests on Love, not on restraint. The government of Ireland by England rests on restraint and not on law; and, since it demands no love, it can evoke no loyalty. Judicial assassination today is reserved only for one race of the King's subjects, for Irishmen; for those who cannot forget their allegiance to the realm of Ireland.

What is the fundamental charter of an Englishman's

liberty? That he shall be tried by his peers. With all respect I assert that this court is to me, an Irishman, a foreign court – this jury is for me, an Irishman, not a jury of my peers.

It is patent to every man of conscience that I have an indefeasible right, if tried at all under this statute of high treason, to be tried in Ireland, before an Irish court, and by an Irish jury.

This court, this jury, the public opinion of this country, England, cannot but be prejudiced in varying degree against me, most of all in time of war. From this court and its jurisdiction I appeal to those I am alleged to have wronged, and to those I am alleged to have injured by my 'evil example,' and claim that they alone are competent to decide my guilt or my innocence.

This is so fundamental a right, so natural a right, so obvious a right, that it is clear the Crown were aware of it when they brought me by force and by stealth from Ireland to this country. It was not I who landed in England, but the Crown who dragged me here, away from my own country, to which I had returned with a price upon my head, away from my own countrymen, whose loyalty is not in doubt, and safe from the judgement of my peers, whose judgement I do not shrink from.

I admit no other judgment but theirs. I accept no verdict save at their hands.

I assert from this dock that I am being tried here not because it is just, but because it is unjust.

[. . .]

But let me say that I am prouder to stand here today in the traitor's dock to answer this impeachment than to fill the place of my accusers. If there be no right of rebellion against a state of things that no savage tribe would endure without resistance, then am I sure that it is better for men to fight and die without right than to live in such a state of right as this.

Where all your rights become only an accumulated wrong; where men must beg with bated breath for leave to subsist in their own land, to think their own thoughts, to sing their own songs, to garner the fruit of their own labours – and even while they beg to see these things inexorably withdrawn from them – then surely it is a braver, a saner, and a truer thing to be a rebel in act and deed against such circumstances as this than tamely to accept it as the natural lot of men.

My Lord, I have done. Gentlemen of the Jury, I wish to thank you for your verdict. I hope you will not think that I made any imputation upon your truthfulness or your integrity when I said that this was not a trial by my peers.

—— THE CONSEQUENCES ——

On 3 August 1916, Roger Casement was hanged for treason. But the British Government was determined not to create any more Irish martyrs. In an effort to smear his name, government officials released the so-called 'black diaries', which told of homosexual dalliances with young men and adolescent prostitutes.

For years, Casement's admirers angrily – and plausibly – claimed that the diaries were fake. In 2002 however, a scientific analysis concluded that they probably are in fact a genuine record of Casement's deeds.

If the science is right, Casement must be regarded as a complex and perhaps deeply flawed individual. But, flawed or not, his final defiant protest against the oppression of his countrymen remains an articulate and powerful defence of Irish Nationalism, and a moving record of an undoubtedly courageous man.

1916
THERE IS NO SALVATION FOR INDIA

MOHANDAS GANDHI
(1869–1948)

Born in Queen Victoria's India, at the height of the British Raj, Mohandas Gandhi's early life exposed him to both sides of the British Empire. In London where, like many of his compatriots, he was training to be a lawyer, Gandhi saw the imperial capital in all its splendour. But, soon after qualifying, he took a legal post in British-ruled South Africa, where he saw colonialism and racism at its worst.

For twenty years, Gandhi was a tireless campaigner for South African civil rights. It was there that he developed his philosophy of *satyagraha*, a doctrine of non-violent resistance that encouraged honesty, co-operation and compassion and deplored more warlike methods of opposition.

Gandhi had a deep impact on South Africa but when he

returned to India in 1915 he was still a relative unknown. However, that would soon change. In 1916, he gave one of his first public speeches in India, to an audience of students, aristocrats and colonial grandees at the opening of a new university at Benares. It was this speech that put Gandhi firmly on the map.

——THE SPEECH——

[. . .]

I want to think audibly this evening. I do not want to make a speech and if you find me this evening speaking without reserve, pray, consider that you are only sharing the thoughts of a man who allows himself to think audibly, and if you think that I seem to transgress the limits that courtesy imposes upon me, pardon me for the liberty I may be taking.

[. . .]

I have turned the searchlight all over, and as you have given me the privilege of speaking to you, I am laying my heart bare. Surely we must set these things right in our progress towards self-government. I now introduce you to another scene. His Highness the Maharaja who presided yesterday over our deliberations spoke about the poverty of India. Other speakers laid great stress upon it. But what did we witness in the great pandal [*a temporary religious structure*] in which the foundation ceremony was performed by the Viceroy? Certainly a most gorgeous show, an exhibition of jewellery, which made a splendid feast for the eyes of the greatest jeweller who chose to come from Paris.

I compare with the richly bedecked noble men the millions of the poor. And I feel like saying to these noble men, 'There is no salvation for India unless you strip yourselves of this jewellery and hold it in trust for your countrymen in India.' I am sure it is not the desire of the King-Emperor ... that in order to show the truest loyalty ... it is necessary for us to ransack our jewellery boxes and to appear bedecked from top to toe. I would undertake, at the peril of my life, to bring to you a message from King George himself that he expects nothing of the kind.

Sir, whenever I hear of a great palace rising in any great city of India, be it in British India or be it in India which is ruled by our great chiefs, I become jealous at once, and say, 'Oh, it is the money that has come from the agriculturists.' Over seventy-five per cent of the population are agriculturists and Mr Higginbotham told us last night in his own felicitous language, that they are the men who grow two blades of grass in the place of one. But there cannot be much spirit of self-government about us, if we take away or allow others to take away from them almost the whole of the results of their labour. Our salvation can only come through the farmer. Neither the lawyers, nor the doctors, nor the rich landlords are going to secure it.

[. . .]

—— THE CONSEQUENCES ——

When Gandhi gave this speech Indian nationalism had been steadily gaining momentum. A generation of highly educated Indians were chafing under the iniquities of British rule. The Indian National Congress, formed in 1885, had been agitating for greater independence from Britain. There had been growing unrest too. In 1912, the Viceroy, Lord Hardinge, had narrowly survived an assassination attempt.

Gandhi agreed that independence was desirable but his approach to winning it was revolutionary. To achieve true independence, he argued, his country would have to prove itself worthy. Instead of turning his 'spotlight' on the British overlords, Gandhi directed it towards India itself.

The glittering princes in the audience were not pleased by his remarks about wealth, extravagance and the common man. Nor did the rest of his speech go much better. Long before he reached his conclusion, Gandhi was hastily hurried from the stage.

But his bold new path to independence did catch on. By the 1920s, Gandhi had become a sort of living saint in India – a popular hero whose every move provoked passion from the people and fear in their colonial masters. In 1947, after decades of struggle, the British finally relinquished their grip. Gandhi, his mission accomplished, was assassinated the following year.

Other Notable Lines

In November 1938, as Japanese troops swept across China, Mao Zedong addressed the Central Committee of the Chinese Communist Party.

The leader's message was simple: Every Communist must grasp the truth – political power grows out of the barrel of a gun.'

They were prophetic words. As the Second World War dragged on, Mao's communist armies grew in strength, fighting an effective guerrilla war against the Japanese invaders. And having defeated the Japanese, he was free, in 1946, to turn on the Kuomintang, a rival Chinese faction.

By 1950, Mao had become ruler of the whole of China. But the power that grew from the gun could not loosen its grip on violence. Mao's peacetime reforms dragged China into the twentieth century, and lie at the root of its current wealth, but millions of Chinese died along the way.

1939
FIRST SOLDIER OF THE GERMAN REICH

ADOLF HITLER
(1889–1945)

No politician in history has used the power of rhetoric to more evil effect than Adolf Hitler. At mass rallies he would whip his audiences into a frenzy – listeners wept and laughed, hanging on every word, shouting their support in great choruses of *Sieg Heil*.

Except for this malign talent, Hitler had little to arm him in his struggle to conquer Germany's soul. He had been an unexceptional student, and had fought as a lowly lance-corporal in the First World War.

But, as Hitler turned to extreme nationalist politics after the war, his ability to play on grievances and stir up anger proved to be an unbeatable weapon. By 1921, he had risen to become leader of what would become the Nazi Party, and his fiery speeches soon attracted more followers to the growing movement.

I HAVE A DREAM

Despite a spell in prison after the failed Munich Putsch, and a subsequent ban on public speaking, Hitler's momentum was unstoppable. In 1933, with his popularity soaring, he was appointed Chancellor of the German Republic. Soon after, through a combination of political bullying and paramilitary violence, he abolished the republic altogether, replacing it with a new 'Third Reich'.

Six years later, on 1 September 1939, with this speech, Hitler announced to his ministers that Germany was going to war with Poland.

——THE SPEECH——

For months we have been suffering under the torture of a problem which the Versailles Diktat created [*the occupation by Poland of the 'Danzig Corridor' after the end of the First World War*] – a problem which has deteriorated until it becomes intolerable for us …

As always, I attempted to bring about, by the peaceful method of making proposals for revision, an alteration of this intolerable position … On my own initiative I have, not once but several times, made proposals for the revision of intolerable conditions. All these proposals, as you know, have been rejected … It was all in vain.

[…]

... I am wrongly judged if my love of peace and my patience are mistaken for weakness or even cowardice. I, therefore, decided last night and informed the British Government that in these circumstances I can no longer find any willingness on the part of the Polish Government to conduct serious negotiations with us.

[. . .]

I am asking of no German man more than I myself was ready throughout four years at any time to do. There will be no hardships for Germans to which I myself will not submit. My whole life henceforth belongs more than ever to my people. I am from now on just first soldier of the German Reich. I have once more put on that coat that was the most sacred and dear to me. I will not take it off again until victory is secured, or I will not survive the outcome.

[. . .]

As a National Socialist and as a German soldier I enter upon this struggle with a stout heart. My whole life has been nothing but one long struggle for my people, for its restoration, and for Germany. There was only one watchword for that struggle: faith in this people. One word I have never learned: that is, surrender.

... I would, therefore, like to assure all the world that

a November 1918 [*Germany's surrender in the First World War*] will never be repeated in German history.

[. . .]

And I would like to close with the declaration that I once made when I began the struggle for power in the Reich. I then said: 'If our will is so strong that no hardship and suffering can subdue it, then our will and our German might shall prevail.'

——THE CONSEQUENCES——

Looked at in hindsight, this speech is an astonishing catalogue of lies. Every undertaking, every solemn declaration, was broken within a few short years. All Hitler's fulminations about imagined grievances were nothing more than a shameless pretext. Germany was being launched into total war.

France and Britain had guaranteed Polish independence. When the Germans attacked, the two Western powers had no choice but to support their ally. In 1941, Germany attacked Russia, despite a secret Nazi–Soviet Pact, signed in August 1939, under which the Soviet Union invaded eastern Poland on 17 September. Later in 1941, the US joined the fight, following the Japanese surprise attack at Pearl Harbor.

Of all the lies in Hitler's speech, the greatest was that Germany's war of aggression would be victorious. By

1945, the vaunted Nazi army had been decimated. Across the world, anything from 60 to 80 million people had been killed. Some 6 million Jews had perished in the genocide of the Holocaust, along with a similar number made up of Slavs, homosexuals, communists, Gypsies and others. As spring arrived in Europe, Soviet troops advanced into the streets of a shattered Berlin.

Far below the burning city, Hitler, knowing he was finished, committed suicide. In that one thing, at least, he kept his word.

Other Notable Lines

Neville Chamberlain was not a bad prime minister. He has, however, had the misfortune to be remembered for his one catastrophic error of judgement.

It was 1938, and Chamberlain had just returned from Germany where he had been meeting Adolf Hitler. At that meeting, Hitler had accepted a deal which gave him control of the German-populated Czech region of the Sudetenland.

Deprived of this mountainous frontier, Czechoslovakia was defenceless before the German war machine, but Hitler had promised that after the Sudetenland, he had no more territorial ambitions in Europe. So, when Chamberlain landed, he brandished his newly signed agreement at the crowds and spoke the oft-misquoted words: 'I believe it is peace for our time.'

1940
THREE WARTIME
SPEECHES

WINSTON CHURCHILL
(1874–1965)

Winston Churchill did not have an auspicious childhood. 'If you cannot prevent yourself', his frustrated father once wrote, 'from leading the idle useless unprofitable life you have had during your schooldays ... you will become a mere social wastrel.'

And as a young man, despite his clear potential, he made as many enemies as friends. The diarist Beatrice Webb, meeting him in 1903, thought him 'egotistical ... shallow-minded and reactionary' – by no means a unique impression.

When, after a successful career as a soldier and war correspondent, he decided to enter politics, his headstrong ways and willingness to speak his mind always held him back from the highest office. Throughout the 1930s, for example, he was a thorn in the side of the government, constantly warning unwilling listeners of the deadly threat posed by the newly powerful Nazi regime.

But when Hitler invaded Czechoslovakia and then Poland in 1939, Churchill was proved suddenly and terrifyingly right. In May 1940, he became prime minister.

He faced a daunting situation. Across the English Channel, British and French forces were being driven back by the Nazis' *Blitzkrieg*. Many in the British establishment were soon contemplating a hasty peace.

But Churchill was defiant. As France crumbled, the Prime Minister deployed his full rhetorical arsenal to rally his people for the struggle ahead.

—— THE SPEECHES ——

BLOOD, TOIL, TEARS AND SWEAT
(HOUSE OF COMMONS, 13 MAY 1940)

This was Churchill's first speech to the Commons as prime minister. The previous night, German troops had crossed into Belgium, the Netherlands and Luxembourg. The Battle of France had begun.

… In this crisis I hope I may be pardoned if I do not address the House [*of Commons*] at any length today. I hope that any of my friends and colleagues, or former colleagues, who are affected by the political reconstruction, will make allowance, all allowance, for any lack of ceremony with which it has been necessary to act. I would say to the House, as I said to those who have joined this government: 'I have nothing to offer but blood, toil, tears and sweat.' We have before us an ordeal of the most grievous kind. We have before us many, many long months of struggle and of suffering. You ask, what is our policy? I can say: It is to wage war, by sea, land and air, with all our might and with all the strength that God can give us; to wage war against a monstrous tyranny, never surpassed in the dark, lamentable catalogue of human crime. That is our policy. You ask, what is our aim? I can answer in one word: It is victory, victory at all costs, victory in spite of all terror, victory, however long and hard the road may be; for without victory, there is no survival. Let that be realized; no survival for the British Empire, no survival for all that the British Empire has stood for, no survival for the urge and impulse of the ages, that mankind will move forward towards its goal. But I take up my task with buoyancy and hope. I feel sure that our cause will not be suffered to fail among men. At this time I feel entitled to claim the aid of all, and I say, 'come then, let us go forward together with our united strength.'

Other Notable Lines

Guiseppe Garibaldi grew up in a divided Italy. A patchwork of small Italian states feuded with each other, or laboured under the rule of foreign masters.

So in 1848, he embarked on a mission to wipe away the fractious old order and create a new Italian republic in its stead.

His initial efforts did not go to plan. In 1849, he found himself in Rome, wounded and defeated, and facing the prospect of surrender to a besieging French army. Defiant, he addressed a crowd in St Peter's Square:

> Soldiers, I am going out from Rome. Let those who wish to continue the war against the stranger, come with me. I offer neither pay, nor quarters, nor provisions. I offer hunger, thirst, forced marches, battles and death. Let him who loves his country follow me.

It took over a decade, but Garibaldi's dream of a unified nation was finally realized, and he is remembered as the father of modern Italy. Years later, Winston Churchill's 'Blood, Toil, Tears and Sweat' speech drew inspiration from Garibaldi's famous words.

WE SHALL FIGHT ON THE BEACHES
(HOUSE OF COMMONS, 4 JUNE 1940)

Churchill delivered this speech not long after the successful evacuation of the British Expeditionary Force from Dunkirk. After a stirring account of the operation, and the heroism of those who made it possible, Churchill continues:

Nevertheless, our thankfulness at the escape of our Army and so many men, whose loved ones have passed through an agonizing week, must not blind us to the fact that what has happened in France and Belgium is a colossal military disaster. The French Army has been weakened, the Belgian Army has been lost, a large part of those fortified lines upon which so much faith had been reposed is gone, many valuable mining districts and factories have passed into the enemy's possession, the whole of the Channel ports are in his hands, with all the tragic consequences that follow from that, and we must expect another blow to be struck almost immediately at us or at France.

[. . .]

Even though large tracts of Europe and many old and famous States have fallen or may fall into the grip of the Gestapo and all the odious apparatus of Nazi rule, we shall not flag or fail. We shall go on to the end, we shall fight in France, we shall fight on the seas and oceans, we shall fight with growing confidence and growing strength in the air, we shall defend our Island, whatever the cost may be, we shall fight on the beaches, we shall fight on the landing grounds, we shall fight in the fields and in the streets, we shall fight in the hills; we shall never surrender, and even if, which I do not for a moment believe, this Island or a large part of it were subjugated and starving, then our Empire beyond the seas, armed and guarded by the British Fleet, would carry on the struggle, until, in God's good time, the New World, with all its power and might, steps forth to the rescue and the liberation of the old.

THEIR FINEST HOUR
(HOUSE OF COMMONS, 18 JUNE 1940)

By the time Churchill made this speech, it had become clear that France was utterly defeated. Churchill spent much of the time trying to be reassuring, talking up the strength of British defences against invasion, but in his ringing conclusion he left no doubt as to what was at stake:

What General Weygand [*the French commander-in-chief*] called the Battle of France is over. I expect that the Battle of Britain is about to begin. Upon this battle depends the survival of Christian civilization. Upon it depends our own British life, and the long continuity of our institutions and our Empire.

The whole fury and might of the enemy must very soon be turned on us. Hitler knows that he will have to break us in this Island or lose the war. If we can stand up to him, all Europe may be free and the life of the world may move forward into broad, sunlit uplands. But if we fail, then the whole world, including the United States, including all that we have known and cared for, will sink into the abyss of a new Dark Age made more sinister, and perhaps more protracted, by the lights of perverted science. Let us therefore brace ourselves to our duties, and so bear ourselves that, if the British Empire and its Commonwealth last for a thousand years, men will still say, 'This was their finest hour.'

—— THE CONSEQUENCES ——

Years earlier, during the First World War, Churchill had written to his wife: 'everything tends towards catastrophe and collapse. I am interested, geared up and happy. Is it not horrible to be built like that?'

Now, in a position of far greater responsibility, and with a far worse disaster looming, he was inspired to new heights and his speeches, broadcast on the BBC, inspired his countrymen.

Britain had every reason to fear Hitler. And the example of France – which surrendered despite having a largely intact navy and huge numbers of men still under arms – had shown the importance of national morale. Within a month of Churchill's 'Finest Hour' speech, the first German bombers had struck at British cities. That August, as Fighter Command struggled to hold off the Luftwaffe, Churchill immortalized the RAF's pilots: 'never in the field of human conflict was so much owed by so many to so few.'

But the country held its nerve. The Battle of Britain was won by the year's end, and slowly the tide began to turn. In November 1942, Churchill was able to comment on the British victory at El Alamein in North Africa: 'this is not the end. It is not even the beginning of the end. But it is, perhaps, the end of the beginning.'

Other Notable Lines

In 1940, the Italian Ambassador to Greece told the Greek leader, Ioannis Metaxas, to surrender. He replied in one word: 'No!'

Not much of a speech, perhaps, but the Greek populace took it up with a will, running through the streets chouting 'No! No! No!' over and over again. Even now, the Greeks still celebrate 'No! day' on 28 October each year, in memory of Metaxas's laconic defiance.

1940
L'APPEL DU 18 JUIN

CHARLES DE GAULLE
(1890–1970)

At the beginning of May 1940, the Republic of France was braced for a German invasion. But although Hitler had invaded Poland in 1939 with worrying ease, the French had every reason to be confident. The Allied forces defending France outnumbered the Germans in tanks, planes and men, and the main Franco-German border was defended by the formidable bunkers of the Maginot Line.

But by the middle of June, the French army had been crushed and humiliated. German Panzers had cut through the Allied lines like a knife through mouldy Roquefort. On 14 June, Paris had fallen, and on the 17th, the French prime minister, Marshal Pétain, declared over the radio that France was ready to surrender.

For some French citizens, who still remembered the

terrible bloodshed of the First World War, Pétain's capitulation came as a tremendous relief. Even subjugation seemed a fair price to avoid the carnage of another Western Front.

But at least one Frenchman disagreed. This was Charles de Gaulle, a middle-ranking general distinguished by a particularly Gallic blend of pride and bloody-mindedness, who had escaped to London in the chaos of the French retreat. The day after Pétain's infamous broadcast, de Gaulle took to the airwaves with his own defiant response.

—— THE SPEECH ——

The leaders who, for many years past, have been at the head of the French armed forces have set up a government. Alleging the defeat of our armies, this government has entered into negotiations with the enemy with a view to bringing about a cessation of hostilities.

[. . .]

But has the last word been said? Must we abandon all hope? Is our defeat final and irremediable?

To those questions I answer – No!

Speaking in full knowledge of the facts, I ask you to

believe me when I say that the cause of France is not lost. The very factors that brought about our defeat may one day lead us to victory.

For, remember this, France does not stand alone. She is not isolated. Behind her is a vast empire, and she can make common cause with the British Empire, which commands the seas and is continuing the struggle. Like England, she can draw unreservedly on the immense industrial resources of the United States.

[. . .]

Today we are crushed by the sheer weight of mechanized force hurled against us, but we can still look to a future in which even greater mechanized force will bring us victory. The destiny of the world is at stake.

I, General de Gaulle, now in London, call on all French officers and men who are at present on British soil, or may be in the future, with or without their arms; I call on all engineers and skilled workmen from the armaments factories who are at present on British soil, or may be in the future, to get in touch with me.

Whatever happens, the flame of French resistance must not and shall not die.

I HAVE A DREAM

—— THE CONSEQUENCES ——

This speech may only have reached a limited audience when it was broadcast, but as word of de Gaulle's defiance spread, escapees from France did indeed arrive in London to join the general's modest, but symbolically important, fighting force.

Others, unable to leave Occupied France, also took his final stirring words to heart. Before long, thousands of French men and women were fighting behind German lines, as part of the increasingly powerful Resistance.

Four years later, Charles de Gaulle entered Paris at the head of his victorious army of Free French. Of course, it was the British and the Americans who had done most of the fighting, but de Gaulle's proud presence allowed the French to see themselves as their own liberators.

De Gaulle was to serve for years as president of France, during which time his country maintained an air of national pride – some might even say superiority – that would have been impossible but for his defiant, intransigent, stand.

1941

Speech on the Anniversary Celebration of the October Revolution

JOSEPH STALIN (1878–1953)

Iosif Vissarionovich Dzhugashvili, as he was born, was the first General Secretary of the Communist Party of the Soviet Union's Central Committee. In his young life Stalin experienced the poverty endured by most peasants in late-nineteenth century Russia but he was a bright child, winning a scholarship to the Tiflis Theological Seminary. Here he joined a secret organization, mixing with social revolutionaries and reading Marxist literature.

Stalin never graduated, instead working as a tutor and a clerk and devoting his evenings to the revolutionary movement. In 1901, he joined the Social Democratic Labour Party, remaining in Russia where he helped to organize industrial resistance to Tsarism. Stalin joined the Bolsheviks in 1903. From then until 1917 he was repeatedly arrested for his political actions and at one point exiled to Siberia.

On his return in 1917 Stalin assisted Lenin in organizing a Bolshevik uprising and was elected General Secretary of the newly named Communist Party in 1922, allowing him to build up a base of support.

After Lenin's death in 1924, Stalin won the power struggle to succeed him and consolidated his support base, outmanoeuvring his political rivals. Now the supreme ruler of the Soviet Union he enforced rapid industrialization, increasing Soviet productivity and economic growth. However, his regime of terror, during which he staged purges that rid the party of 'enemies of the people', resulted in the execution of thousands and the suffering of millions more who were forced into exile.

These purges severely depleted the Red Army and, when Germany invaded Russia on 22 June 1941, Stalin was caught off guard. His ruthlessness won through, and in a series of speeches he rallied the population, calling for a scorched-earth policy that would deny the Germans any supplies. In this speech, given in Red Square on 7 November 1941, the anniversary of the October Revolution, Stalin shows that he is prepared to fight the Germans and that neither he, nor the army, would give in.

—— THE SPEECH ——

Comrades, Red Army and Red Navy men, commanders and political instructors, men and women workers, men and women collective farmers, intellectuals, brothers and sisters in the enemy rear who have temporarily fallen under the yoke of the German brigands, our glorious men and women guerrillas who are disrupting the rear of the German invaders!

On behalf of the Soviet Government and our Bolshevik Party I greet you and congratulate you on the 24th anniversary of the great October Socialist Revolution.

Comrades, today we must celebrate the 24th anniversary of the October Revolution in difficult conditions. The German brigands' treacherous attack and the war that they forced upon us have created a threat to our country. We have temporarily lost a number of regions, and the enemy is before the gates of Leningrad and Moscow.

The enemy calculated that our army would be dispersed at the very first blow and our country forced to its knees. But the enemy wholly miscalculated. Despite temporary reverses, our army and our navy are bravely beating off enemy attacks along the whole front, inflicting heavy losses, while our country – our whole country – has organized itself into a single fighting camp in order, jointly with our army and navy, to rout the German invaders.

There was a time when our country was in a still more difficult position. Recall the year 1918, when we celebrated the first anniversary of the October Revolution. At that time three-quarters of our country was in the hands of foreign interventionists. We had temporarily lost the Ukraine, the Caucasus, Central Asia, the Urals, Siberia and the Far East. We had no allies, we had no Red Army – we had only just begun to create it – and we experienced a shortage of bread, a shortage of arms, a shortage of equipment.

At that time 14 states were arrayed against our country, but we did not become despondent or downhearted. In the midst of the conflagration of war we organized the Red Army and converted our country into a military camp. The spirit of the great Lenin inspired us at that time for the war against the interventionists. And what happened? We defeated the interventionists, regained all our lost territories and achieved victory.

Today our country is in a far better position than it was 23 years ago. Today it is many times richer in industry, food and raw materials. Today we have allies who jointly with us form a united front against the German invaders. Today we enjoy the sympathy and support of all the peoples of Europe fallen under the yoke of Fascist tyranny. Today we have a splendid army and a splendid navy, defending the freedom and independence of our country with their lives. We experience no serious shortage either of food or of arms or equipment.

[. . .]

Is it possible, then, to doubt that we can and must gain victory over the German invaders? The enemy is not as strong as some terror-stricken pseudo-intellectuals picture him. The devil is not as terrible as he is painted. Who can deny that our Red Army has more than once put the much-vaunted German troops to panicky flight?

[. . .]

The German invaders are straining their last forces. There is no doubt that Germany cannot keep up such an effort for any long time. Another few months, another half year, one year perhaps – and Hitlerite Germany must collapse under the weight of its own crimes.

Comrades, Red Army and Red Navy men, commanders and political instructors, men and women guerrillas!

The whole world is looking to you as a force capable of destroying the brigand hordes of German invaders. The enslaved peoples of Europe under the yoke of the German invaders are looking to you as their liberators. A great mission of liberation has fallen to your lot. Be worthy of this mission! The war you are waging is a war of liberation, a just war. Let the heroic images of our great ancestors [. . .] inspire you in this war!

Let the victorious banner of the great Lenin fly over your heads!

Utter destruction to the German invaders!

Death to the German armies of occupation!

Long live our glorious motherland, her freedom and her independence!

Under the banner of Lenin – onward to victory!

—— THE CONSEQUENCES ——

The troops went straight from Red Square to the front. The army held out and, in the north, the Germans were brought to a halt. Stalin called for a counter-attack, despite doubts from his commanders.

On 5 December the Red Army commenced the strategic counter-offensive operation in a period known as the Winter Campaign, pushing the Germans away from the capital. By early January they had been forced back over 150 miles. By staging a series of repetitive offensives, often using fresh soldiers, Stalin proved that the *blitzkrieg* could be thwarted. His approach set an example to troops throughout the world.

Leningrad and Stalingrad, both besieged, held out despite terrible casualties and appalling privations. In February 1943 the entire German army at Stalingrad surrendered; later that year, at Kursk, Russian armour won a convincing victory over the Panzers, and the German forces began to retreat, harried all the way by the Red Army, which eventually, in April/May 1945, captured Berlin.

Hitler's decision to invade the Soviet Union was probably the single most catastrophic mistake in twentieth-century history. But the Soviet Union's redoutable defence was not without its cost: its war dead from the Second World War, civilian and military, are thought to have been more than 23 million, or 14% of its population.

1941

A DATE WHICH WILL
LIVE IN INFAMY

FRANKLIN DELANO ROOSEVELT
(1882–1945)

When American radar operators spotted a large formation of unknown aeroplanes approaching the naval base at Pearl Harbor, Hawaii, they were right to be alarmed. The Second World War was raging in Europe and things in the Pacific were heating up. Diplomats and codebreakers had been warning for months that Japan might break the peace with the USA, that the expansionist Japanese military might attempt a surprise attack.

But when the sighting was reported to the radar information centre at Fort Shafter, the duty officer told the operators not to worry. A flight of friendly bombers was expected that day and was the only plausible explanation for the unusual blip on the radar screens. Surely the Japanese, for all their daring, would never risk so bold a strike so far from their own territory?

Hours later, that same duty officer watched in horror as hundreds of Japanese fighters and dive bombers swarmed out of the summer sky to devastate the lines of US capital ships that lay anchored in the harbour. By the end of the attack, more than 2,000 US servicemen had lost their lives.

The next day, President Franklin Delano Roosevelt addressed the US Congress, giving a speech that would etch itself forever onto America's national consciousness.

—— THE SPEECH ——

Mr Vice President, and Mr Speaker, and Members of the Senate and House of Representatives:

Yesterday, December 7, 1941 – a date which will live in infamy – the United States of America was suddenly and deliberately attacked by naval and air forces of the Empire of Japan.

The United States was at peace with that Nation and, at the solicitation of Japan, was still in conversation with its Government and its Emperor looking toward the maintenance of peace in the Pacific. Indeed, one hour after Japanese air squadrons had commenced bombing in the American Island of Oahu, the Japanese Ambassador to the United States and his colleague delivered to our Secretary of State a formal reply to a recent American message. And while this reply stated that it seemed useless to continue the existing diplomatic negotiations, it contained no threat or hint of war or of armed attack.

It will be recorded that the distance of Hawaii from Japan makes it obvious that the attack was deliberately planned many days or even weeks ago. During the intervening time the Japanese Government has deliberately sought to deceive the United States by false statements and expressions of hope for continued peace.

The attack yesterday on the Hawaiian Islands has caused severe damage to American naval and military forces. I regret to tell you that very many American lives have been lost. In addition American ships have been reported torpedoed on the high seas between San Francisco and Honolulu.

Yesterday the Japanese Government also launched an attack against Malaya.

Last night Japanese forces attacked Hong Kong.

Last night Japanese forces attacked Guam.

Last night Japanese forces attacked the Philippine Islands.

Last night the Japanese attacked Wake Island. And this

morning the Japanese attacked Midway Island. Japan has, therefore, undertaken a surprise offensive extending throughout the Pacific area. The facts of yesterday and today speak for themselves. The people of the United States have already formed their opinions and well understand the implications to the very life and safety of our Nation.

As Commander in Chief of the Army and Navy I have directed that all measures be taken for our defence.

But always will our whole Nation remember the character of the onslaught against us.

No matter how long it may take us to overcome this premeditated invasion, the American people in their righteous might will win through to absolute victory. I believe that I interpret the will of the Congress and of the people when I assert that we will not only defend ourselves to the uttermost but will make it very certain that this form of treachery shall never again endanger us.

Hostilities exist. There is no blinking at the fact that our people, our territory, and our interests are in grave danger.

With confidence in our armed forces – with the unbounding determination of our people – we will gain the inevitable triumph, so help us God. I ask that the Congress declare that since the unprovoked and dastardly attack by Japan on Sunday, December 7, 1941, a state of war has existed between the United States and the Japanese Empire.

—— THE CONSEQUENCES——

By attacking Pearl Harbor, Japan had won a stunning tactical victory. At the same time, however, the country had ensured its own inevitable defeat. America had been unwilling to join the war. Isolationist sentiment was widespread and powerful. But confronted with the photographs of burning battleships, and the lists of dead sailors, the previously unwilling populace hurled itself into battle.

Roosevelt's speech was stern and simple – a perfect expression of a new-found national resolve. America's 'righteous might', he said, and 'unbounding determination', would bring 'absolute victory'.

And though the fight was hard, the balance soon began to swing America's way. At the Battle of Midway, six months later, American airmen had their revenge, crippling the Japanese carrier fleet. US Marines began to push back the Japanese advances in the Pacific. Meanwhile, deep in rural New Mexico, a group of scientists were building the weapon that would repay the debt of Pearl Harbour a thousand-fold.

In August 1945, the Americans dropped an atom bomb

on the Japanese city of Hiroshima, followed soon after by another on Nagasaki. Days later, Japan offered an unconditional surrender.

Other Notable Lines

J. Robert Oppenheimer has the ambiguous distinction of being remembered in history as the father of the atom bomb. He was a brilliant scientist and an ambitious man. He was deeply curious about whether the bomb could be made to work and was pleased when it did.

But he was not a fool. He knew that the device that he and his team at Los Alamos had put together was something both miraculous and awful. In a television broadcast years later, he recalled how he had felt as he watched the first successful bomb test – a quote that would go down in history:

'We knew the world would not be the same. A few people laughed, a few people cried, most people were silent. I remembered the line from the Hindu scripture, the Bhagavad-Gita: "Now, I am become Death, the destroyer of worlds". I suppose we all thought that one way or another.'

1944

Speech on
St Crispin's Day

LAURENCE OLIVIER (1907–1989);
WILLIAM SHAKESPEARE
(*c*.1564–1616)

Of all the speeches in this book, the St Crispin's Day speech from Shakespeare's *Henry V* is the one that took the strangest route to its place in history.

Written around the end of the sixteenth century, the play is a dramatic retelling of the story of King Henry V of England and his campaign leading up to the battle of Agincourt.

In Shakespeare's version of the story, the King leads his band of rugged yeomen to France, faces the flower of French chivalry, and, at Agincourt, humbles a superior force of proud Gallic knights by dint of fine archery, English grit and a particularly stirring eve-of-battle speech.

For nearly three-and-a-half centuries after it was written, the speech was of only literary interest. But in the

1940s, as Britain confronted the Nazis across the English Channel, the old words acquired an unusual new life as wartime propaganda.

At the heart of this resurrection was Laurence Olivier, the country's finest Shakespearian actor, who recited the speech for a BBC radio broadcast in 1942. On the strength of that recording a film version was commissioned, with Olivier in the title role. It hit cinemas in 1944, just as British troops were, like Henry's men, once again fighting in France.

—— THE SPEECH ——

[*Henry has just overheard his cousin wishing for more soldiers*]

What's he that wishes so?
My cousin Westmoreland? No, my fair cousin;
If we are mark'd to die, we are enow
To do our country loss; and if to live,
The fewer men, the greater share of honour.
God's will! I pray thee, wish not one man more.
By Jove, I am not covetous for gold,
Nor care I who doth feed upon my cost;
It yearns me not if men my garments wear;
Such outward things dwell not in my desires.
But if it be a sin to covet honour,
I am the most offending soul alive.
No, faith, my coz, wish not a man from England.
God's peace! I would not lose so great an honour

As one man more methinks would share from me
For the best hope I have. O, do not wish one more!
Rather proclaim it, Westmoreland, through my host,
That he which hath no stomach to this fight,
Let him depart; his passport shall be made,
And crowns for convoy put into his purse;
We would not die in that man's company
That fears his fellowship to die with us.
This day is call'd the feast of Crispian.
He that outlives this day, and comes safe home,
Will stand a tip-toe when this day is nam'd,
And rouse him at the name of Crispian.
He that shall live this day, and see old age,
Will yearly on the vigil feast his neighbours,
And say 'To-morrow is Saint Crispian.'
Then will he strip his sleeve and show his scars,
And say 'These wounds I had on Crispian's day.'
Old men forget; yet all shall be forgot,
But he'll remember, with advantages,
What feats he did that day. Then shall our names,
Familiar in his mouth as household words–
Harry the King, Bedford and Exeter,
Warwick and Talbot, Salisbury and Gloucester–
Be in their flowing cups freshly rememb'red.
This story shall the good man teach his son;
And Crispin Crispian shall ne'er go by,
From this day to the ending of the world,
But we in it shall be remembered–
We few, we happy few, we band of brothers;
For he to-day that sheds his blood with me

Shall be my brother; be he ne'er so vile,
This day shall gentle his condition;
And gentlemen in England now-a-bed
Shall think themselves accurs'd they were not here,
And hold their manhoods cheap whiles any speaks
That fought with us upon Saint Crispin's day.

—— THE CONSEQUENCES ——

Shakespeare's speech is a masterpiece, a perfect example of
the rhetorician's art, and in Olivier's hands, the film was a
huge success. As director as well as star, he masterfully
filleted the play of some of its darker and more ambiguous
moments, leaving a patriotic pageant that stirred the hearts
of all who saw it.

Forty-five years later, and in a very different Britain,
Kenneth Branagh would direct and star in a very different
film of the same play, this time emphasizing the horror, not
the honour, of war. But it is Olivier's Oscar-winning
performance that went down in history. Astride his horse
on St Crispin's Day, Laurence Olivier's King Henry V
remains to this day a defining portrait of wartime valour.

Other Notable Lines

Among William Shakespeare's many wonderful plays, perhaps his most quoted and best-known speech features in *Julius Caesar*, Act III.

Mark Antony is giving a eulogy at the funeral of Julius Caesar. Brutus, one of Caesar's killers, controls Rome, and Antony must be careful how he speaks. But, from the great first line ('Friends, Romans, countrymen, lend me your ears') he has the crowd eating from his hand.

His repeated ironic refrain, 'Brutus is an honourable man,' is the ultimate example of an old rhetorical art: to praise your enemy to the skies and, in doing so, stab him in the back.

1944
SPEECH BEFORE D-DAY

GENERAL GEORGE S. PATTON
(1885-1945)

O ne of the greatest and most colourful generals of
The Second World War was the American George
S. Patton. He had served with distinction on the Western
Front in 1917, in North Africa in 1942 and in Sicily in
1943. By 1944, he was a hugely respected leader and was
entrusted with command of the US Third Army in the
run-up to the Allied invasion of Occupied France.

Patton had a reputation as a straight-talking soldier, and
it was one he delighted in living up to. While British
propaganda chiefs were busily putting the finishing
touches to their inspiring production of *Henry V*, Patton
adopted a rather different tone. On the eve of D-Day he
gathered his men and gave the following speech:

I HAVE A DREAM

—— THE SPEECH——

… You are here today for three reasons. First, because you are here to defend your homes and your loved ones. Second, you are here for your own self respect, because you would not want to be anywhere else.

Third, you are here because you are real men and all real men like to fight …

[. . .]

Sure, we want to go home. We want this war over with. The quickest way to get it over with is to go get the bastards who started it. The quicker they are whipped, the quicker we can go home. The shortest way home is through Berlin and Tokyo. And when we get to Berlin I am personally going to shoot that paper hanging son-of-a-bitch Hitler. Just like I'd shoot a snake!

[. . .]

We're not going to just shoot the sons-of-bitches, we're going to rip out their living Goddamned guts and use them to grease the treads of our tanks. We're going to murder those lousy Hun cocksuckers by the bushel-fucking-basket. War is a bloody, killing business. You've got to spill their blood, or they will spill yours. Rip them up the belly. Shoot them in the guts. When shells are hitting all around you and you wipe the dirt off your face and realize that instead of dirt it's the blood and guts of what once was your best friend beside you, you'll know what to do!

I don't want to get any messages saying, 'I am holding my position.' We are not holding a Goddamned thing. Let the Germans do that. We are advancing constantly and we are not interested in holding onto anything, except the enemy's balls. We are going to twist his balls and kick the living shit out of him all of the time. Our basic plan of operation is to advance and to keep on advancing regardless of whether we have to go over, under, or through the enemy. We are going to go through him like crap through a goose; like shit through a tin horn!

[. . .]

There is one great thing that you men will all be able to say after this war is over and you are home once again. You may be thankful that twenty years from now when you are sitting by the fireplace with your grandson on your knee and he asks you what you did in the great World War II, you won't have to cough, shift him to the other knee and say, 'Well, your Granddaddy shovelled shit in Louisiana.' No, Sir, you can look him straight in the eye and say, 'Son, your Granddaddy rode with the Great Third Army and a

Son-of-a-Goddamned–Bitch named Georgie Patton!'
—— THE CONSEQUENCES ——

The US Third Army didn't arrive in Normandy until one month after D-Day, but when Patton landed, he soon proved that he meant what he had said. His troops burst through the German lines, sweeping through France and encircling two Nazi Panzer Armies on the way. By January 1945, the Third Army had fought more divisions, and moved further and faster than any US Army ever had before.

That spring, the army thrust its way into Germany and Austria and in April, Berlin fell. But Patton never did get to shoot Hitler – the dictator pre-empted him, committing suicide in his hidden bunker on 30 April while Soviet troops fought through the streets above.

Of course, for all his fine speechifying, Patton shouldn't take all the credit for the Third Army's success. 'Old Blood and Guts' was his nickname, but, as his men jokingly pointed out, it was '*our* blood, *his* guts'.

1947

A Tryst with Destiny

JAWAHARLAL NEHRU
(1889–1964)

B y the beginning of the 1940s, Britain had realized that its days of Empire in India were coming to an end. A tiny island nation, bankrupted by the Second World War, could no longer hope to control a subcontinent of a quarter of a billion people.

And those countless millions were becoming ever more difficult to rule. Mohandas Gandhi's non-violent resistance had embarrassed the British overlords. More dangerous yet, the old imperial glue that had joined India's diverse peoples together was coming rapidly unstuck, as Muslims and Hindus clashed violently in the streets.

So, in 1947, a new British Viceroy, the dashing Admiral Lord Louis Mountbatten, arrived in Delhi to get Britain out of India. Five months later, the deed was done, and India declared independence.

The first man to try to lead this newly created nation was Jawaharlal Nehru, an aristocratic politician, and a veteran of India's long struggle for freedom. Nehru was a fierce believer in Indian independence, but he was also, in many respects, every bit the elegant English gentleman, educated at Harrow and Cambridge and trained in law at London's Inner Temple. On the night of 14 August, as his country prepared for independence, Nehru made the following speech:

—— THE SPEECH ——

Long years ago we made a tryst with destiny, and now the time comes when we shall redeem our pledge, not wholly or in full measure, but very substantially. At the stroke of the midnight hour, when the world sleeps, India will awake to life and freedom. A moment comes, which comes but rarely in history, when we step out from the old to the new, when an age ends, and when the soul of a nation, long suppressed, finds utterance.

[. . .]

The appointed day has come – the day appointed by destiny – and India stands forth again, after long slumber and struggle, awake, vital, free and independent. The past clings on to us still in some measure and we have to do much before we redeem the pledges we have so often taken. Yet the turning point is past, and history begins anew for us, the history which we shall live and act and others will write about.

It is a fateful moment for us in India, for all Asia and for the world. A new star rises, the star of freedom in the east, a new hope comes into being, a vision long cherished materializes. May the star never set and that hope never be betrayed! We rejoice in that freedom, even though clouds surround us, and many of our people are sorrow-stricken and difficult problems encompass us. But freedom brings responsibilities and burdens and we have to face them in the spirit of a free and disciplined people.

[. . .]

We are citizens of a great country, on the verge of bold advance, and we have to live up to that high standard. All of us, to whatever religion we may belong, are equally the children of India with equal rights, privileges and obligations. We cannot encourage communalism or narrow-mindedness, for no nation can be great whose people are narrow in thought or in action.

To the nations and peoples of the world we send greetings and pledge ourselves to cooperate with them in furthering peace, freedom and democracy.

And to India, our much-loved motherland, the ancient, the eternal and the ever-new, we pay our reverent homage and we bind ourselves afresh to her service. Jai Hind!

—— THE CONSEQUENCES ——

Amid the 'trysts with destiny' and 'stars of freedom', Nehru had carefully sounded a more cautious note, warning of the 'difficult problems' that lay ahead.

Sadly, his fears were fully realized. The same Act of Parliament that gave India independence had also, at the urging of the powerful Muslim League, divided the old British dominion into two new countries: Hindu India and Muslim Pakistan.

On the day of Partition, millions of refugees crossed the newly drawn borders. As they passed through hostile communities, unrest became full-blown civil war, with massacres carried out on both sides. Hundreds of thousands were killed.

However, more than half a century later, India is emerging from poverty to become one of the world's major democratic powers. Despite the pitfalls and problems, and the continuing tensions with Pakistan, Nehru's idealistic vision of India is slowly being fulfilled.

1960
WINDS OF CHANGE

HAROLD MACMILLAN
(1894–1986)

In the decades following the Second World War, it became clear that the age of empire was over. India was independent. South East Asia had launched its own struggle against colonialism. And in Africa, almost all of which was controlled by one or other of the European powers, a new generation of educated black nationalists was coming to the fore, demanding freedom after centuries of white rule.

Through the fifties and sixties, more and more of these African countries got their way. The great swaths of British pink that covered the continent on schoolroom maps gave way to a patchwork of newly independent nations.

In 1960, as this movement was at its height, the British Prime Minister, Harold Macmillan, travelled to South Africa. The Republic had been independent since 1931 but, for the substantial black majority, this had not led to any sort of liberation. Instead, a white colonial elite enforced a strict segregationist policy of 'apartheid' (meaning 'separateness') that subjected the country's black citizens to repressive legalized discrimination.

Arriving in Cape Town, Macmillan addressed a state that was still deeply wedded to the racist legacy of the past. His task was to open its eyes to the new reality of the present.

—— THE SPEECH ——

... Ever since the break-up of the Roman Empire one of the constant facts of political life in Europe has been the emergence of independent nations. They have come into existence over the centuries in different forms, different kinds of government, but all have been inspired by a deep, keen feeling of nationalism, which has grown as the nations have grown ...

Today the same thing is happening in Africa, and the most striking of all the impressions I have formed since I left London a month ago is of the strength of this African national consciousness. In different places it takes different forms, but it is happening everywhere.

The wind of change is blowing through this continent, and whether we like it or not, this growth of national consciousness is a political fact. We must all accept it as a fact, and our national policies must take account of it.

Well you understand this better than anyone, you are sprung from Europe, the home of nationalism, here in Africa you have yourselves created a free nation. A new nation. Indeed in the history of our times yours will be recorded as the first of the African nationalists. This tide of national consciousness which is now rising in Africa, is a fact, for which both you and we, and the other nations of the western world are ultimately responsible.

For its causes are to be found in the achievements of western civilisation, in the pushing forwards of the frontiers of knowledge, the applying of science to the service of human needs, in the expanding of food production, in the speeding and multiplying of the means of communication, and perhaps above all and more than anything else in the spread of education.

As I have said, the growth of national consciousness in Africa is a political fact, and we must accept it as such. That means, I would judge, that we've got to come to terms with it. I sincerely believe that if we cannot do so we may imperil the precarious balance between the East and West on which the peace of the world depends ...

Macmillan was a Conservative politician of the old school, educated at Eton, steeped in the mannerisms of the traditional ruling class. But although his message was delivered with typical patrician charm, it concealed a severe rebuke. As Douglas Hurd, a former Conservative Foreign Secretary, later wrote, when Macmillan said 'of course, you understand this better than anyone', he really meant: 'you need to understand this more than anyone, but I doubt you do'.

South Africa, it was strongly implied, had fallen behind the times. Not only that – by failing to provide a good example of Western values in action, it risked driving the new nations of Africa towards the chilly embrace of the Soviet bloc and disastrously upsetting the precarious balance of Cold War power.

Sadly, South Africa refused to heed Macmillan's warning. Apartheid remained central to the country's policy for a further three decades, leaving it economically backward and politically isolated. But Macmillan's speech did send out an important signal to the rest of Africa. Despite the old bonds of friendship between the two nations, Britain would not stand with South Africa in resisting the 'wind of change'.

Other Notable Lines

Some time around the year AD 83, the Roman general Gnaeus Agricola was extending Rome's empire to its furthest limits. An arduous march had taken his legions to northern Scotland. There they met the Caledonians, led by their king, Calgacus.

The Romans won a predictable victory and returned south. The unremarkable battle would be worthy of little attention were it not for the speech which the Roman historian Tacitus puts into the mouth of the Caledonian king – one of history's earliest, and most powerful, condemnations of imperialism. Most enduring is one famous line: 'They [the Romans] plunder, they slaughter, and they steal: this they falsely name Empire, and where they make a wasteland, they call it peace.'

1961
INAUGURAL ADDRESS

PRESIDENT JOHN F. KENNEDY
(1917–1963)

John Fitzgerald Kennedy certainly overcame his share of
challenges on his way to the US presidency. As a naval
officer in the Second World War his patrol boat was sunk by
a Japanese destroyer; he floated in the sea for three days
before he was saved. As a young congressman he was dogged
by illness (a rare endocrine disorder called Addison's
Disease); steroid injections finally saved his career.

Far more formidable obstacles lay in wait simply by
virtue of his birth. For one thing, he was extraordinarily
young for a presidential candidate. And, even worse, he was
Catholic. With the Cold War reaching a climax, any ill-
defined sense that Kennedy was in some way 'un-
American' could have been fatal.

But, by the narrowest of margins, Kennedy won the
presidential elections of 1960. Now he had to win over the

American people. Coming into a political sphere dominated by aged white Protestants (President Eisenhower, the incumbent, was the oldest man ever to have held the office), Kennedy, in his inaugural address, took his perceived weaknesses and turned them into strengths, presenting himself as part of a new fresh generation.

—— THE SPEECH ——

Fellow citizens:

We observe today not a victory of party but a celebration of freedom – symbolizing an end as well as a beginning – signifying renewal as well as change. For I have sworn before you and Almighty God the same solemn oath our forebears prescribed nearly a century and three-quarters ago.

The world is very different now. For man holds in his mortal hands the power to abolish all forms of human poverty and all forms of human life. And yet the same revolutionary beliefs for which our forebears fought are still at issue around the globe – the belief that the rights of man come not from the generosity of the state but from the hand of God.

We dare not forget today that we are the heirs of that first revolution. Let the word go forth from this time and place, to friend and foe alike, that the torch has been passed to a new generation of Americans – born in this century, tempered by war, disciplined by a hard and bitter peace, proud of our ancient heritage – and unwilling to witness or permit the slow undoing of those human rights to which this nation has always been committed, and to which we are committed today at home and around the world.

Let every nation know, whether it wishes us well or ill, that we shall pay any price, bear any burden, meet any hardship, support any friend, oppose any foe to assure the survival and the success of liberty.

This much we pledge – and more.

To those old allies whose cultural and spiritual origins we share, we pledge the loyalty of faithful friends ...

To those new states whom we welcome to the ranks of the free, we pledge our word that one form of colonial control shall not have passed away merely to be replaced by a far more iron tyranny ...

To those people in the huts and villages of half the globe struggling to break the bonds of mass misery, we pledge our best efforts to help them help themselves, for whatever period is required ... If a free society cannot help the many who are poor, it cannot save the few who are rich.

To our sister republics south of our border, we offer a special pledge – to convert our good words into good deeds – in a new alliance for progress – to assist free men and free governments in casting off the chains of poverty ...

To that world assembly of sovereign states, the United Nations, our last best hope in an age where the instruments of war have far outpaced the instruments of peace, we renew our pledge of support ...

Finally, to those nations who would make themselves our adversary, we offer not a pledge but a request: that both sides begin anew the quest for peace, before the dark powers of destruction unleashed by science engulf all humanity in planned or accidental self-destruction.

[...]

In the long history of the world, only a few generations have been granted the role of defending freedom in its hour of maximum danger. I do not shrink from this responsibility – I welcome it. I do not believe that any of us would exchange places with any other people or any other generation. The energy, the faith, the devotion which we bring to this endeavor will light our country and all who serve it – and the glow from that fire can truly light the world.

And so, my fellow Americans: ask not what your country can do for you – ask what you can do for your country.

My fellow citizens of the world: ask not what America will do for you, but what together we can do for the freedom of man …

—— THE CONSEQUENCES ——

Kennedy came to power at a time of huge global challenges. The Cold War had reached new and perilous heights. In June 1961, Kennedy endured a difficult meeting with his Soviet counterpart Nikita Khruschev, who dominated the young president, warning that communism would 'bury' the capitalist West.

Soon, construction started on the Berlin Wall, separating capitalist West Berlin from the Soviet East. The US-sponsored Bay of Pigs invasion of Cuba was a miserable failure. A massively expanded programme of Soviet missile tests escalated the nuclear arms race.

Most challenging of all was the Cuban missile crisis of 1962. For a few tense days, Kennedy and Khrushchev were locked in a battle of wills over the presence of nuclear missiles just a few hundred miles off the American coast. The world seemed on the brink of an annihilating nuclear war.

In those dark days, Kennedy's speech stood as a shining declaration of intent – a bold statement that the USA had what it took to overcome all challenges. For 1,037 days, until he was assassinated by Lee Harvey Oswald in 1963, Kennedy led his nation through one of the toughest periods in American history. He remains among the country's most celebrated presidents.

Other Notable Lines

On 20 July 1969, the world held its breath as a fragile craft holding two American astronauts approached the barren surface of Earth's moon. At last, the Eagle lander touched down on the dry rock. From the inside of the lunar module, Neil Armstrong radioed back to NASA in Texas. 'Houston, Tranquillity Base here. The Eagle has landed.'

There were still hours of preparation to do before the astronauts could open the Eagle's hatch. But at last, on 21 July, Neil Armstrong stepped out of the cramped module into the vacuum of space. Slowly, he climbed down the ladder and, as his foot touched the lunar dust, he spoke his famous words: 'That's one small step for man. One giant leap for mankind.'

1963
I HAVE A DREAM

MARTIN LUTHER KING
(1929–1968)

In 1863, Abraham Lincoln's Emancipation Proclamation ended American slavery in the Unionist northern states. Two years later, with the Civil War over and the slave-owning Confederacy defeated, the captive millions toiling in the southern cotton fields looked forward to a new dawn of freedom.

For a while, it looked like that dawn had come. Despite violent objection in the South, the occupying federal troops protected the black population's right to freedom, and the vote.

But in 1877, the troops withdrew, leaving the South in the hands of radical Democrat politicians called 'the Redeemers'. Black voters were prevented from registering. Racist paramilitaries like the Ku Klux Klan formed lynch mobs. Before long, a string of segregation laws had designated 'whites only' train carriages, cafes, drinking fountains and waiting rooms.

Into this apartheid USA was born Martin Luther King Jr. As the son of a respected Baptist preacher and civil rights activist, it was no surprise when young Martin announced an 'inner urge' to 'serve God and humanity'. By 1955 he had a doctorate in theology and had followed his father into the Church.

By 1963, Dr King, with his ringing preacher's tones and knack for rhetoric, had become a leader of the growing civil rights movement, demanding an end to segregation and legal discrimination. So it was that he found himself, late that summer, facing a vast crowd in Washington, where, under the shadow of the Lincoln Memorial, he gave the following extraordinary speech.

—— THE SPEECH ——

[. . .]

Five score years ago, a great American, in whose symbolic shadow we stand today, signed the Emancipation Proclamation. This momentous decree came as a great beacon light of hope to millions of Negro slaves who had been seared in the flames of withering injustice. It came as a joyous daybreak to end the long night of their captivity.

But one hundred years later, the Negro still is not free. One hundred years later, the life of the Negro is still sadly crippled by the manacles of segregation and the chains of discrimination … And so we've come here today to dramatize a shameful condition.

[*King continued with his prepared speech. It was powerful stuff, laden with references to the Founding Fathers and the Constitution – a blazing tirade at the injustices suffered by his people. Finally, having said his piece, he reached his intended conclusion:*]

[. . .]

I am not unmindful that some of you have come here out of great trials and tribulations. Some of you have come fresh from narrow jail cells. And some of you have come from areas where your quest – quest for freedom left you battered by the storms of persecution and staggered by the winds of police brutality. You have been the veterans of creative suffering. Continue to work with the faith that unearned suffering is redemptive. Go back to Mississippi, go back to Alabama, go back to South Carolina, go back to Georgia, go back to Louisiana, go back to the slums and ghettos of our northern cities, knowing that somehow this situation can and will be changed.

[*At around this point, as King was about to sit down, the soul singer Mahalia Jackson called to him from the crowd: 'Tell them about your dream, Martin. Tell them about the dream.' Hearing her, King began to extemporize and it is at this point that the speech really comes alive.*]

Let us not wallow in the valley of despair, I say to you today, my friends.

And so even though we face the difficulties of today and tomorrow, I still have a dream. It is a dream deeply rooted in the American dream.

I have a dream that one day this nation will rise up and live out the true meaning of its creed: 'We hold these truths to be self-evident, that all men are created equal.'

I have a dream that one day on the red hills of Georgia, the sons of former slaves and the sons of former slave owners will be able to sit down together at the table of brotherhood.

I have a dream that one day even the state of Mississippi, a state sweltering with the heat of injustice, sweltering with the heat of oppression, will be transformed into an oasis of freedom and justice.

I have a dream that my four little children will one day live in a nation where they will not be judged by the colour of their skin but by the content of their character.

I have a dream today!

I have a dream that one day, down in Alabama, with its vicious racists, with its governor having his lips dripping with the words of 'interposition' and 'nullification' – one day right there in Alabama little black boys and black girls will be able to join hands with little white boys and white girls as sisters and brothers.

I have a dream today!

I have a dream that one day every valley shall be exalted, and every hill and mountain shall be made low, the rough places will be made plain, and the crooked places will be made straight; 'and the glory of the Lord shall be revealed and all flesh shall see it together'.

This is our hope, and this is the faith that I go back to the South with.

With this faith, we will be able to hew out of the mountain of despair a stone of hope. With this faith, we will be able to transform the jangling discords of our nation into a beautiful symphony of brother-hood. With this faith, we will be able to work together, to pray together, to struggle together, to go to jail together, to stand up for freedom together, knowing that we will be free one day.

And this will be the day – this will be the day when all of God's children will be able to sing with new meaning:

My country 'tis of thee, sweet land of liberty, of thee I sing.

Land where my fathers died, land of the Pilgrim's pride,

From every mountainside, let freedom ring!

And if America is to be a great nation, this must become true.

And so let freedom ring from the prodigious hilltops of New Hampshire.

Let freedom ring from the mighty mountains of New York.

Let freedom ring from the heightening Alleghenies of Pennsylvania.

Let freedom ring from the snow-capped Rockies of Colorado.

Let freedom ring from the curvaceous slopes of California.

But not only that:

Let freedom ring from Stone Mountain of Georgia.

Let freedom ring from Lookout Mountain of Tennessee.

Let freedom ring from every hill and molehill of Mississippi.

From every mountainside, let freedom ring.

And when this happens, when we allow freedom ring, when we let it ring from every village and every hamlet, from every state and every city, we will be able to speed up that day when all of God's children, black men and white men, Jews and Gentiles, Protestants and Catholics, will be able to join hands and sing in the words of the old Negro spiritual:

Free at last! Free at last!
Thank God Almighty, we are free at last!

I HAVE A DREAM

—— THE CONSEQUENCES ——

Dr King's speech was a milestone in America's struggle for civil rights. His fiery words, which blended intellectual argument, biblical rhetoric and patriotic exhortation ('let freedom ring' turns the words of a famous patriotic song into something that is almost a prayer), gave new heart to the advocates of black equality.

Just as important, it forced the politicians in Washington to sit up and take notice. In 1964, the US government finally passed the Civil Rights Act, officially ending segregation. A year later, the Voting Rights Act ended the disenfranchisement of African Americans.

But this was not the end of the struggle. Discrimination was still rife. Many black activists, disillusioned, were rejecting King's non-violent precepts in favour of a more militant kind of struggle.

By 1968, King's influence was on the wane, but he remained optimistic. 'It doesn't matter with me now,' he said, in a speech to his followers, 'because I've been to the mountaintop and I've seen the Promised Land. I may not get there with you. But I want you to know tonight, that we, as a people, will get to the Promised Land.'

The next day, standing on the balcony of a Memphis hotel, Martin Luther King was shot and killed by a white segregationist. He was thirty-nine years old.

1964
THE BALLOT OR
THE BULLET

MALCOLM X
(1925–1965)

While Martin Luther King sought equality for African Americans through non-violent protest, a darker, more ambiguous movement was growing in the shadows. Its most famous figurehead was the Islamic activist Malcolm X.

Born in Nebraska as plain old Malcolm Little, this future leader excelled at school, but ended up in prison after a combination of home tragedy and prejudice sent his life off the rails.

While behind bars, he discovered religion and, when he was paroled in 1952, he reinvented himself as Malcolm X, minister of the Nation of Islam, a black nationalist Muslim sect. The 'X' was a symbol for his lost African name, stolen from his ancestors by their slavemasters.

Malcolm X forcefully denounced Martin Luther King's

peaceful campaigns. 'Revolution is bloody,' he once said. 'Revolution is hostile, revolution knows no compromise, revolution overturns and destroys everything that gets in its way.'

But by 1964, he had started to soften his position. He rejected the Nation of Islam, specifically its belief that whites were 'devils', and started to advocate political, rather than militant, activism. In April that year, at a Methodist Church in Ohio, he laid out his new philosophy in what would become perhaps his most famous speech.

—— THE SPEECH ——

... The question tonight, as I understand it, is 'The Negro Revolt, and Where Do We Go From Here?' or 'What Next?' In my little humble way of understanding it, it points toward either the ballot or the bullet.

[. . .]

... All of us have suffered here, in this country, political oppression at the hands of the white man, economic exploitation at the hands of the white man, and social degradation at the hands of the white man.

Now in speaking like this, it doesn't mean that we're anti-white, but it does mean we're anti-exploitation, we're anti-degradation, we're anti-oppression. And if the white man doesn't want us to be anti-him, let him stop oppressing and exploiting and degrading us …

If we don't do something real soon, I think you'll have to agree that we're going to be forced either to use the ballot or the bullet. It's one or the other in 1964. It isn't that time is running out – time has run out!

[. . .]

I'm not a politician, not even a student of politics; in fact, I'm not a student of much of anything. I'm not a Democrat. I'm not a Republican, and I don't even consider myself an American. If you and I were Americans, there'd be no problem. Those Honkies that just got off the boat, they're already Americans; Polacks are already Americans; the Italian refugees are already Americans. Everything that came out of Europe, every blue-eyed thing, is already an American. And as long as you and I have been over here, we aren't Americans yet.

[*There follows a long explanation of the current state of American politics. Malcolm X says that black votes have been wasted, allowing southern segregationist Democrats – or 'Dixiecrats' – to block civil rights legislation. Properly co-ordinated, he says, the black vote could be a powerful weapon. Finally, he reaches this conclusion:*]

I say again, I'm not anti-Democrat, I'm not anti-Republican, I'm not anti-anything. I'm just questioning their sincerity, and some of the strategy that they've been using on our people by promising them promises that they don't intend to keep. When you keep the Democrats in power, you're keeping the Dixiecrats in power. I doubt that my good Brother Lomax will deny that. A vote for a Democrat is a vote for a Dixiecrat. That's why, in 1964, it's time now for you and me to become more politically mature and realize what the ballot is for; what we're supposed to get when we cast a ballot; and that if we don't cast a ballot, it's going to end up in a situation where we're going to have to cast a bullet. It's either a ballot or a bullet.

— THE CONSEQUENCES —

Malcolm X's simple style could hardly be more different from the high-flown rhetoric of Martin Luther King. Nevertheless, the speech did strike a chord with his oppressed and disenfranchised audience.

Whether it advanced the cause of civil rights is another matter. By speaking about 'bullets', Malcolm X did little to build trust between the races. But the aggressive talk may have had a hidden benefit. Malcolm X himself is reported to have said: 'if the white people realize what the alternative is, perhaps they will be more willing to hear Dr King.'

In 1965, the Voting Rights Act ended all legal

disenfranchisement of African Americans. The ballot, not the bullet, would be the preferred weapon during the ongoing struggle for equality. But Malcolm X was not alive to see it. Like Martin Luther King, he was assassinated, shot in the chest in 1965 by vengeful members of his own old organization, the Nation of Islam.

Other Notable Lines

A great speech can be amazingly powerful – but there are times when words just won't do. One man who understood this perfectly was the German Chancellor Willy Brandt who, in 1970, travelled to Poland to attend a memorial for the victims of the Warsaw Ghetto.

Thousands of Jews had been murdered here by the Nazis. 'Nowhere else', as Brandt later recalled, 'had a people suffered as in Poland. The machine-like annihilation of Polish Jewry represented a heightening of bloodthirstiness that no one had held possible.'

So when the ceremony came, Brandt found that words failed him. Instead, in perfect silence, he fell to his knees and bowed his head. His act of penitence opened the painful way to reconciliation.

1980
THE LADY'S NOT
FOR TURNING

MARGARET THATCHER
(1 9 2 5 –)

In the British general election of 1979, a greengrocer's daughter from Lincolnshire made history by becoming the UK's first female prime minister.

Her name was Margaret Thatcher, and she was a new kind of Conservative politician. She came, unlike many of her predecessors, from a modest background, brought up in a flat above her family's shop – an upbringing that gave her a life-long respect for what might have been called 'bourgeois' values: self-reliance, patriotism, entrepreneurialism.

But when Thatcher came to power after the financial crises of the 1970s, these qualities seemed in short supply. Britain, stripped of its colonies, rocked by recession and suffering from severe inflation, was a nation in decline – a once imperial power adjusting painfully to its diminished status in the new world order.

To try to reverse this slide, Thatcher put in place a series of harsh fiscal measures aimed at reducing inflation. However, this caused rising unemployment and popular discontent, which then led to widespread media speculation about a possible 'U-turn'. Characteristically, at the 1980 Conservative Party conference, Thatcher took the opportunity to address the doubters head-on.

—— THE SPEECH ——

[. . .]

It is sometimes said that because of our past we, as a people, expect too much and set our sights too high. That is not the way I see it. Rather it seems to me that throughout my life in politics our ambitions have steadily shrunk. Our response to disappointment has not been to lengthen our stride but to shorten the distance to be covered. But with confidence in ourselves and in our future what a nation we could be!

[. . .]

[*Thatcher now lists some of her party's economic accomplishments. She then continues:*]

But all this will avail us little unless we achieve our prime economic objective – the defeat of inflation. Inflation destroys nations and societies as surely as invading armies do. Inflation is the parent of unemployment. It is the unseen robber of those who have saved.

[. . .]

...some people talk as if control of the money supply [*to combat inflation*] was a revolutionary policy. Yet it was an essential condition for the recovery of much of continental Europe.

Those countries knew what was required for economic stability. Previously, they had lived through rampant inflation...

Today, after many years of monetary self-discipline, they have stable, prosperous economies better able than ours to withstand the buffeting of world recession.

[. . .]

[*European leaders ask:*] 'Has Britain the courage and resolve to sustain the discipline for long enough to break through to success?'

Yes, Mr Chairman, we have, and we shall. This Government are determined to stay with the policy and see it through to its conclusion. That is what marks this administration as one of the truly radical ministries of post-war Britain. Inflation is falling and should continue to fall.

Meanwhile we are not heedless of the hardships and worries that accompany the conquest of inflation. Foremost among these is unemployment. Today our country has more than 2 million unemployed. Now you can try to soften that figure in a dozen ways ... But when all that has been said the fact remains that the level of unemployment in our country today is a human tragedy ... The waste of a country's most precious assets – the talent and energy of its people – makes it the bounden duty of Government to seek a real and lasting cure.

[. . .]

If spending money like water was the answer to our country's problems, we would have no problems now. If ever a nation has spent, spent, spent and spent again, ours has. Today that dream is over. All of that money has got us nowhere but it still has to come from somewhere. Those who urge us to relax the squeeze, to spend yet more money indiscriminately in the belief that it will help the unemployed and the small businessman are not being kind or compassionate or caring.

[. . .]

If our people feel that they are part of a great nation and they are prepared to will the means to keep it great, a great nation we shall be, and shall remain. So, what can stop us from achieving this? What then stands in our way? The prospect of another winter of discontent? I suppose it might.

But I prefer to believe that certain lessons have been learnt from experience – that we are coming, slowly, painfully, to an autumn of understanding. And I hope that it will be followed by a winter of common sense. If it is not, we shall not be diverted from our course.

To those waiting with bated breath for that favourite media catchphrase, the 'U' turn, I have only one thing to say. 'You turn if you want to. The lady's not for turning.'

[. . .]

… So let us resist the blandishments of the faint hearts; let us ignore the howls and threats of the extremists; let us stand together and do our duty, and we shall not fail.

Extracts reproduced with permission from www.margaretthatcher.org, the website of the Margaret Thatcher Foundation where the full text can be found.

—— THE CONSEQUENCES ——

Even today, more than twenty years after she left power, Margaret Thatcher remains perhaps the most divisive prime minister in British history. To her supporters she was a visionary, single-handedly stopping Britain's plunge towards mediocrity. To her critics, she was a cold-hearted ideologue, who ravaged Britain's industrial heart and brought in a new social order in which greed was the only good.

Britain's economy came through the pain of mass unemployment to reach the boom years of the 1980s, before crashing again in 1991, but how much responsibility Thatcher's policies should take for either boom or bust is hotly disputed.

Yet, however controversial, her economic legacy has left an indelible mark on British history – the state-run industries and highly regulated markets of the 1970s were swept away, leaving today's modern capitalist society in their place.

1987
TEAR DOWN
THIS WALL!

PRESIDENT RONALD REAGAN
(1911–2004)

In 1937, Warner Brothers Studios in California offered a screen test to a handsome young man named Ronald Reagan. The trial was a success, and from the late thirties to the mid-sixties, Reagan starred in a succession of modestly successful Hollywood films. He later described himself as the 'Errol Flynn of the B-movies'.

But although his acting career never quite brought him real stardom, it was an invaluable preparation for his future career on the greater stage of global politics. Elected governor of California in 1967, Reagan used often to recycle lines from his own movies in political speeches.

When he became president in 1980, Reagan found himself playing the lead in one of the twentieth century's most compelling dramas: the final decay of the Soviet Union. A climactic moment came in 1987, in Berlin – a city divided between the communist East and the capitalist West by the notorious Berlin Wall.

New Soviet policies of openness and freedom had led to hopes that the communist regime might finally be relaxing its iron grip. In front of a crowd of thousands of West Germans, and knowing his speech was being watched in the East, Reagan issued the Soviet leader, Mikhail Gorbachev, a ringing challenge.

—— THE SPEECH ——

[. . .]

Our gathering today is being broadcast throughout Western Europe and North America. I understand that it is being seen and heard as well in the East. To those listening throughout Eastern Europe, I extend my warmest greetings and the good will of the American people. To those listening in East Berlin, a special word: Although I cannot be with you, I address my remarks to you just as surely as to those standing here before me. For I join you, as I join your fellow countrymen in the West, in this firm, this unalterable belief: Es gibt nur ein Berlin. [*There is only one Berlin.*]

Behind me stands a wall that encircles the free sectors of this city, part of a vast system of barriers that divides the entire continent of Europe. From the Baltic, south, those barriers cut across Germany in a gash of barbed wire, concrete, dog runs, and guardtowers ... a restriction on the right to travel ... an instrument to impose upon ordinary men and women the will of a totalitarian state.

Yet it is here in Berlin where the wall emerges most clearly; here, cutting across your city, where the news photo and the television screen have imprinted this brutal division of a continent upon the mind of the world. Standing before the Brandenburg Gate, every man is a German, separated from his fellow men. Every man is a Berliner, forced to look upon a scar.

... Yet I do not come here to lament. For I find in Berlin a message of hope, even in the shadow of this wall, a message of triumph.

[...]

In West Germany and here in Berlin, there took place an economic miracle ...

Where four decades ago there was rubble, today in West Berlin there is the greatest industrial output of any city in Germany ...

Where a city's culture seemed to have been destroyed, today there are two great universities, orchestras and an opera, countless theatres, and museums.

Where there was want, today there's abundance – food, clothing, automobiles – the wonderful goods of the Ku'damm. From devastation, from utter ruin, you Berliners have, in freedom, rebuilt a city that once again ranks as one of the greatest on Earth ...

In the 1950s, Khrushchev predicted: 'We will bury you.' But in the West today, we see a free world that has achieved a level of prosperity and wellbeing unprecedented in all human history.

In the Communist world, we see failure, technological backwardness, declining standards of health, even want of the most basic kind – too little food. Even today, the Soviet Union still cannot feed itself. After these four decades, then, there stands before the entire world one great and inescapable conclusion: Freedom leads to prosperity. Freedom replaces the ancient hatreds among the nations with comity and peace. Freedom is the victor.

And now the Soviets themselves may, in a limited way, be coming to understand the importance of freedom. We hear much from Moscow about a new policy of reform and openness. Some political prisoners have been released. Certain foreign news broadcasts are no longer being jammed. Some economic enterprises have been permitted to operate with greater freedom from state control. Are these the beginnings of profound changes in the Soviet state?

Or are they token gestures, intended to raise false hopes in the West, or to strengthen the Soviet system without changing it? We welcome change and openness; for we believe that freedom and security go together, that the advance of human liberty can only strengthen the cause of world peace.

There is one sign the Soviets can make that would be unmistakable, that would advance dramatically the cause of freedom and peace. General Secretary Gorbachev, if you seek peace, if you seek prosperity for the Soviet Union and Eastern Europe, if you seek liberalization: Come here to this gate! Mr Gorbachev, open this gate! Mr Gorbachev, tear down this wall!

[. . .]

As I looked out a moment ago from the Reichstag, that embodiment of German unity, I noticed words crudely spray-painted upon the wall, perhaps by a young Berliner, 'This wall will fall. Beliefs become reality.' Yes, across Europe, this wall will fall. For it cannot withstand faith; it cannot withstand truth. The wall cannot withstand freedom.

[. . .]

Thank you and God bless you all.

I HAVE A DREAM

—— THE CONSEQUENCES ——

The Berlin Wall had separated East and West Berlin since 1961. Thousands of East Berliners, desperate to escape to a better life in the West, had crossed it – some through tunnels, others by leaping out of the windows of apartment buildings, or even with the help of light aircraft or hot air balloons.

Hundreds had died in the attempt. In the most notorious case, in 1962, an eighteen-year-old boy was shot just a few metres from the West German border. Unable to help him, Western border guards watched in horror as he bled to death from his wounds.

But, in 1989, two years after Reagan's dramatic speech, a wave of popular protest on the East German side brought the hated barrier crashing down. The East Germans opened the Berlin border crossings and, within days, swarms of ordinary people armed with picks and hammers had reduced much of the wall to rubble.

Symbolically, this marked the end of communist rule in Eastern Europe. Just like the wall, Soviet-backed regimes across the region crumbled. The Iron Curtain, which had split the continent for more than four decades, was lifted at last.

Other Notable Lines

Bucharest, 1989. Nicolae Ceauşescu, the hated Romanian dictator, was condemning an earlier outbreak of unrest at the town of Timisoara.

In his arrogance, he was broadcasting live, in front of a press-ganged crowd. But, to his horror, the mood soon began to turn. Suddenly, the whole crowd could be clearly heard over the live broadcast, chanting their *support* of the Timisoara protesters.

Confronted by this unprecedented display of defiance, Ceauşescu froze, and although the censors pulled the plug on the broadcast moments later, the damage was done. The next day, encouraged by his weakness, the people stormed the palace and toppled his regime.

1990
FREEDOM FROM FEAR

AUNG SAN SUU KYI
(1945–)

Born in Rangoon, in Burma, Aung San Suu Kyi was raised by her mother, after her father was assassinated by political rivals in 1947. From an early age, Suu Kyi was surrounded by people of varying backgrounds, religions and politics, and her own mother was prominent in the newly formed Burmese government. Politically aware, and well educated in New Delhi and Oxford, she went on to work for the United Nations in New York.

Suu Kyi returned to Burma in 1988 to look after her ailing mother, but soon became involved in the country's democracy movement. On 8 August that year, a mass demonstration for democracy was violently suppressed and a new military junta seized power. In response, Suu Kyi and some fellow campaigners formed the National League for Democracy (NLD), for which they were placed under house arrest on 20 July 1989.

I HAVE A DREAM

In 1990, facing extreme domestic and international pressure, the dictatorship was forced to call a general election. The NLD won 80% of the parliamentary seats, a result which the ruling generals refused to recognize.

In the same year, Suu Kyi was awarded the Sakharov Prize for Freedom of Thought and, in 1991, the Nobel Peace Prize. The following speech was given in 1991, in acceptance of the former.

—— THE SPEECH ——

It is not power that corrupts but fear. Fear of losing power corrupts those who wield it and fear of the scourge of power corrupts those who are subject to it … With so close a relationship between fear and corruption it is little wonder that in any society where fear is rife corruption in all forms becomes deeply entrenched.

[…]

The effort necessary to remain uncorrupted in an environment where fear is an integral part of everyday existence is not immediately apparent to those fortunate enough to live in states governed by the rule of law. Just laws do not merely prevent corruption by meting out impartial punishment to offenders. They also help to create a society in which people can fulfil the basic requirements necessary for the preservation of human dignity without recourse to corrupt practices. Where there are no such laws, the burden of upholding the principles of justice and common decency falls on the ordinary people. It is the cumulative effect on their sustained effort and steady endurance which will change a nation where reason and conscience are warped by fear into one where legal rules exist to promote man's desire for harmony and justice while restraining the less desirable destructive traits in his nature.

[. . .]

The wellspring of courage and endurance in the face of unbridled power is generally a firm belief in the sanctity of ethical principles combined with a historical sense that despite all setbacks the condition of man is set on an ultimate course for both spiritual and material advancement. It is his capacity for self-improvement and self-redemption which most distinguishes man from the mere brute. At the root of human responsibility is the concept of perfection, the urge to achieve it, the intelligence to find a path towards it, and the will to follow that path if not to the end at least the distance needed to rise above individual limitations and environmental impediments. It is man's vision of a world fit for rational, civilized humanity which leads him to dare and to suffer to build societies free from want and fear. Concepts such as truth, justice and compassion cannot be dismissed as trite when these are often the only bulwarks which stand against ruthless power.

—— THE CONSEQUENCES ——

Since giving this speech, Aung San Suu Kyi has been in and out of arrest and refused visits from her family. Drawing strength from her Buddhist faith she remains as committed to her cause as ever. Thousands of Burmese political prisoners have drawn inspiration from her words and, though the campaign to liberate all campaigners for democracy continues, international pressure has ensured degrees of freedom to many.

While she was temporarily allowed to travel in 2003, an assassination attempt was made on Suu Kyi's life as members of the Union Solidarity and Development Association (USDA), formed by the military junta, brutally attacked a convoy of vehicles. Suu Kyi reached safety but more than fifty of her fellow NLD supporters were savagely beaten to death in what is known as the Depayin Massacre. Suu Kyi was placed under house arrest again.

Throughout 2009, diplomatic visits by the US, coupled with pressure from various international governments and organizations, forced the Burmese government to consider the release of all its political captives. A court ruling in August set an expiry date for Suu Kyi's imprisonment.

On the evening of 13 November 2010, Aung San Suu Kyi was released from house arrest. Thousands of her supporters gathered outside her home in Rangoon to witness the removal of barricades. Many wore T-shirts emblazoned with the slogan 'We stand with Aung San Suu Kyi'. Suu Kyi had been detained for fifteen of the past twenty-one years.

1994
LET FREEDOM REIGN

NELSON MANDELA
(1918–)

Raised by tribal royalty in a small village in South Africa's Eastern Cape Province, Nelson Mandela endured years of oppression to become his country's first black president, and one of the most respected statesmen of modern times.

In 1943, he joined the African National Congress (ANC), established some thirty years earlier to protest against the injustices of the apartheid regime, which oppressed the country's black majority through a series of stringent segregation laws.

Mandela soon became a high-profile activist within the movement. In 1960, after sixty-nine protesters were killed by white police in the Sharpeville Massacre, Mandela and the ANC embarked on a campaign of economic sabotage, using bombs to destroy power-lines and government offices (although they were careful to avoid causing casualties).

The campaign did not last long. In 1963, he was arrested and sentenced to five years for leaving the country illegally. While in prison he was tried for sabotage, defiantly declaring at his trial that freedom was 'an ideal for which I am prepared to die'. He was given a life sentence.

In the end his death was not required as a price for freedom. In 1990, under mounting international pressure, the South African government released Mandela from prison where he had suffered for twenty-seven years. In May 1994, he was elected president of a new, free, South Africa. This is his inaugural speech.

—— THE SPEECH ——

Your Majesties, Your Royal Highnesses, distinguished guests, comrades and friends,

Today, all of us do, by our presence here, and by our celebrations in other parts of our country and the world, confer glory and hope to newborn liberty.

Out of the experience of an extraordinary human disaster that lasted too long, must be born a society of which all humanity will be proud.

Our daily deeds as ordinary South Africans must produce an actual South African reality that will reinforce humanity's belief in justice, strengthen its confidence in the nobility of the human soul and sustain all our hopes for a glorious life for all. All this we owe both to ourselves and to the peoples of the world who are so well represented here today.

To my compatriots, I have no hesitation in saying that each one of us is as intimately attached to the soil of this beautiful country as are the famous jacaranda trees of Pretoria and the mimosa trees of the bushveld. Each time one of us touches the soil of this land, we feel a sense of personal renewal. The national mood changes as the seasons change. We are moved by a sense of joy and exhilaration when the grass turns green and the flowers bloom.

That spiritual and physical oneness we all share with this common homeland explains the depth of the pain we all carried in our hearts as we saw our country tear itself apart in terrible conflict, and as we saw it spurned, outlawed and isolated by the peoples of the world, precisely because it has become the universal base of the pernicious ideology and practice of racism and racial oppression.

We, the people of South Africa, feel fulfilled that humanity has taken us back into its bosom, that we, who were outlaws not so long ago, have today been given the rare privilege to be host to the nations of the world on our own soil.
We thank all our distinguished international guests

for having come to take possession with the people of our country of what is, after all, a common victory for justice, for peace, for human dignity.

We trust that you will continue to stand by us as we tackle the challenges of building peace, prosperity, non-sexism, non-racialism and democracy …

The time for the healing of the wounds has come.

The moment to bridge the chasms that divide us has come.

The time to build is upon us.

We have, at last, achieved our political emancipation. We pledge ourselves to liberate all our people from the continuing bondage of poverty, deprivation, suffering, gender and other discrimination.

We succeeded to take our last steps to freedom in conditions of relative peace. We commit ourselves to the construction of a complete, just and lasting peace. We have triumphed in the effort to implant hope in the breasts of the millions of our people. We enter into a covenant that we shall build the society in which all South Africans, both black and white, will be able to walk tall, without any fear in their hearts, assured of their inalienable right to human dignity – a rainbow nation at peace with itself and the world …

We dedicate this day to all the heroes and heroines in this country and the rest of the world who sacrificed in many ways and surrendered their lives so that we could be free. Their dreams have become reality. Freedom is their reward.

We are both humbled and elevated by the honour and privilege that you, the people of South Africa, have bestowed on us, as the first president of a united, democratic, non-racial and non-sexist South Africa, to lead our country out of the valley of darkness.

We understand it still that there is no easy road to freedom. We know it well that none of us acting alone can achieve success. We must therefore act together as a united people, for national reconciliation, for nation building, for the birth of a new world.

Let there be justice for all. Let there be peace for all. Let there be work, bread, water and salt for all. Let each know that for each the body, the mind and the soul have been freed to fulfil themselves.

Never, never and never again shall it be that this beautiful land will again experience the oppression of one by another and suffer the indignity of being the skunk of the world. The sun shall never set on so glorious a human achievement.

Let freedom reign. God bless Africa.

—— THE CONSEQUENCES ——

Defenders of apartheid had long argued that if black South Africans were given the vote, it would be 'one man, one vote, one time'. White South Africans, they feared, would be permanently disenfranchised, and a dysfunctional regime would soon put an end to dreams of true democracy.

And indeed South Africa's path to freedom was not without dangers, even after the end of apartheid. Much of the populace was desperately poor, angry and marginalized by decades of discrimination. The hunger for democracy could easily have been overwhelmed by the thirst for revenge.

Fortunately, in Mandela, the country had a leader of truly inspiring vision. In speeches like his inaugural address, he drove the message home that this was a new dawn for *all* South Africans, not a revolution by some at the expense of others.

Today in the 'Rainbow Nation', despite its deeply entrenched social problems, freedom still does reign.

Other Notable Lines

In his 1995 film epic *Braveheart,* Mel Gibson gave the world one of the most imitated, and most parodied, speeches to have come out of recent fiction.

Resplendent with long hair and (anachronistic) blue face-paint, Gibson, playing the part of William Wallace, addresses his army of loyal Scots:

Fight and you may die. Run and you will live – at least awhile. And dying in your bed many years from now, would you be willing to trade all the days from this day to that for one chance, just one chance, to come back here as young men and tell our enemies that they may take our lives but they will never take our freedom!

2001

DECLARATION OF
WAR ON THE
UNITED STATES

OSAMA BIN LADEN
(1957–2011)

G enerous and softly spoken, at least according to those
who have met him, Osama bin Laden makes an
unlikely terrorist. The man who has topped the US most
wanted list for a decade was born into luxury, the
seventeenth son of a Yemeni construction magnate living
in Saudi Arabia.

But in the 1980s, bin Laden abandoned worldly
distractions to fight against Soviet invaders in Afghanistan.
Backed by the CIA, among others, he established a camp for
Islamic warriors in the border provinces of Pakistan. This
camp was simply named 'the base', or, in Arabic, *Al Qaeda*.

The holy war, or *jihad*, in Afghanistan was a resounding
success, and bin Laden sought a new direction for his pious
wrath. When infidel US troops established bases on the

sacred soil of Saudi Arabia before the first Gulf War of 1991, America presented the perfect target.

Throughout the late nineties, bin Laden produced a string of violent tirades and *fatwas* against the American 'crusaders'. But it was not until 2001, with the devastating 9/11 attack on the World Trade Centre in New York, that he found himself with a truly global audience.

—— THE SPEECH ——

[...]

What the United States tastes today is a very small thing compared to what we have tasted for tens of years. Our nation has been tasting this humiliation and contempt for more than eighty years. Its sons are being killed, its blood is being shed, its holy places are being attacked, and it is not being ruled according to what God has decreed.

Despite this, nobody cares.

[...]

One million Iraqi children have thus far died in Iraq although they did not do anything wrong ...

Israeli tanks and tracked vehicles also enter to wreak havoc in Palestine, in Jenin, Ramallah, Rafah, Beit

Jala, and other Islamic areas and we hear no voices raised or moves made.

But if the sword falls on the United States after eighty years, hypocrisy raises its head lamenting the deaths of these killers who tampered with the blood, honour and holy places of the Muslims.

The least that one can describe these people is that they are morally depraved.

They champion falsehood, support the butcher against the victim, the oppressor against the innocent child.

May God mete them the punishment they deserve.

[. . .]

These incidents divided the entire world into two regions – one of faith where there is no hypocrisy and another of infidelity, from which we hope God will protect us.

The winds of faith and change have blown to remove falsehood from the [*Arabian*] peninsula of Prophet Mohammed, may God's prayers be upon him.

As for the United States, I tell it and its people these few words: I swear by Almighty God who raised the heavens without pillars that neither the United States nor he who lives in the United States will enjoy security before we can see it as a reality in Palestine and before all the infidel armies leave the land of Mohammed, may God's peace and blessing be upon him.

[. . .]

— THE CONSEQUENCES —

This message was broadcast on the Arabic news channel Al Jazeera, one month after the fall of the Twin Towers. Bin Laden sits cross-legged in a dark cave dressed in a turban and army fatigues, with an AK47 propped against the rock wall behind him.

The rhetoric is stark. Two weeks earlier, George Bush had said, 'either you are with us, or you are with the terrorists'. Bin Laden expresses the same opinion in reverse when he splits the world into 'two regions', thus setting the stage for a global confrontation.

Once, his words would have been dismissed as empty threats. But with 9/11, he had proved that he could and would convert word into deed and realize his bloody ambition of an implacable war against the West.

This speech taught the world to believe that it was not dealing with criminals, but with holy warriors. The response, therefore, was war – a war which, a decade later, is still being waged. Bin Laden himself remains at large.

2002
THE AXIS OF EVIL

PRESIDENT GEORGE W. BUSH
(1946–)

The 9/11 attacks on the World Trade Centre in New York in 2001 stunned America. For the first time since Pearl Harbor, a foreign enemy had taken American lives on American soil, shattering the comforting illusions of US isolationism.

The response came within a month. US and British forces invaded Afghanistan and toppled the terrorist-harbouring Taliban regime. It was a bold statement of American power – the long arm of international law reaching across continents into Central Asia's dark heart to pluck out a festering abscess of hostile intent.

Against this backdrop of US victory, President George W. Bush prepared to make his 2002 State of the Union Address. He was not an exceptional public speaker, better known for blunt certainty than rhetorical sophistication, but this speech proved to be one of American history's defining moments.

— THE SPEECH —

… For many Americans, these four months have brought sorrow, and pain that will never completely go away.

Every day a retired firefighter returns to Ground Zero, to feel closer to his two sons who died there.

At a memorial in New York, a little boy left his football with a note for his lost father: Dear Daddy, please take this to Heaven. I don't want to play football until I can play with you again some day.

Last month, at the grave of her husband, Michael, a CIA officer and Marine who died in Mazur-e-Sharif, Shannon Spann said these words of farewell: 'Semper Fi, my love.' Shannon is with us tonight.

Shannon, I assure you and all who have lost a loved one that our cause is just, and our country will never forget the debt we owe Michael and all who gave their lives for freedom.

[. . .]

Our cause is just, and it continues …

What we have found in Afghanistan confirms that, far from ending there, our war against terror is only beginning. Most of the 19 men who hijacked planes on September the 11th were trained in Afghanistan's camps, and so were tens of thousands of others. Thousands of dangerous killers, schooled in the methods of murder, often supported by outlaw regimes, are now spread throughout the world like ticking time bombs, set to go off without warning.

[. . .]

My hope is that all nations will heed our call, and eliminate the terrorist parasites who threaten their countries and our own …

But some governments will be timid in the face of terror. And make no mistake about it: If they do not act, America will.

Our … goal is to prevent regimes that sponsor terror from threatening America or our friends and allies with weapons of mass destruction. Some of these regimes have been pretty quiet since September the 11th. But we know their true nature. North Korea is a regime arming with missiles and weapons of mass destruction, while starving its citizens.

Iran aggressively pursues these weapons and exports terror, while an unelected few repress the Iranian people's hope for freedom.

Iraq continues to flaunt its hostility toward America and to support terror. The Iraqi regime has plotted to develop anthrax, and nerve gas, and nuclear weapons for over a decade. This is a regime that has already used poison gas to murder thousands of its own citizens – leaving the bodies of mothers huddled over their dead children. This is a regime that agreed to international inspections – then kicked out the inspectors. This is a regime that has something to hide from the civilized world.

States like these, and their terrorist allies, constitute an axis of evil, arming to threaten the peace of the world. By seeking weapons of mass destruction, these regimes pose a grave and growing danger. They could provide these arms to terrorists, giving them the means to match their hatred. They could attack our allies or attempt to blackmail the United States. In any of these cases, the price of indifference would be catastrophic.

... All nations should know: America will do what is necessary to ensure our nation's security.

[...]

Our war on terror is well begun, but it is only begun. This campaign may not be finished on our watch – yet it must be and it will be waged on our watch.

[. . .]

—— THE CONSEQUENCES ——

As soon as Bush uttered the words 'axis of evil' they started reverberating around the halls of Western power, the almost biblical rhetoric sitting most uneasily with the urbane technocrats of Europe. Chris Patten, the EU's Foreign Affairs chief, warned of the dangers of 'absolutist positions'. The French Foreign Minister, Hubert Vedrine, tutted about a new 'simplism'.

But the speech was a hit with the crowd back home. The wounds of 9/11 still bit deep. Perhaps Afghanistan had been almost too easy and they needed a grand crusade to rid the world of dark forces.

Bush's words laid the foundation for nearly a decade of US military involvement in the Middle East. Even now, US troops are still fighting in Afghanistan, and Iraq is still torn by terrorist insurgency.

Ironically, the campaign that Bush launched with his bellicose address revealed not America's strength but rather the limits of its global reach. Acting unilaterally in the Middle East, the world's most powerful nation found its resources severely and unexpectedly stretched.

Other Notable Lines

George Bush celebrated the official end of combat operations in Iraq with a victory speech aboard the USS *Abraham Lincoln*, one of the great aircraft carriers that had been deployed to the Gulf.

And yet, despite the occasion, few long remembered what he said. There was no 'axis of evil' soundbite to resound through the free world.

What they did remember, with cruel frequency, as US casualties mounted over the succeeding years, was the banner that fluttered jauntily behind him: a Stars and Stripes, bearing the words 'Mission Accomplished'.

2003
EVE OF BATTLE
SPEECH

COLONEL TIM COLLINS
(1960–)

The second Gulf War opened in 2003 against a background of fear, anger and uncertainty. In Britain, Tony Blair was urging the importance of invading Iraq to secure Saddam Hussein's alleged weapons of mass destruction. Saddam supported terrorists, he warned. To leave his regime unchanged would risk devastating attacks on British cities.

But on London's streets, tens of thousands of demonstrators disagreed. Blair's name bobbed on protest banners above the heads of vast crowds. He was, they shouted, a lying British lapdog, pantingly following his cowboy master into an unwise and unjust war.

Meanwhile, in the Arabian Desert, British troops waited anxiously for the order to invade. Among them was Colonel Tim Collins, an Ulsterman serving with the

Royal Irish Regiment and veteran of the SAS, with more than twenty years' service. His determination and character had earned him the respect of his men – who called him 'Nails' – but little in the way of public recognition.

That was about to change. As the day of the attack approached, Collins assembled his men and, without notes, delivered his eve of battle address.

—— THE SPEECH ——

We go to liberate, not to conquer. We will not fly our flags in their country. We are entering Iraq to free a people and the only flag which will be flown in that ancient land is their own. Show respect for them.

There are some who are alive at this moment who will not be alive shortly. Those who do not wish to go on that journey, we will not send. As for the others, I expect you to rock their world. Wipe them out if that is what they choose.

But if you are ferocious in battle remember to be magnanimous in victory. Iraq is steeped in history. It is the site of the Garden of Eden, of the Great Flood and the birthplace of Abraham. Tread lightly there.

You will see things that no man could pay to see – and you will have to go a long way to find a more decent, generous and upright people than the Iraqis. You will be embarrassed by their hospitality even though they have nothing. Don't treat them as refugees for they are in their own country ... In years to come they will know that the light of liberation in their lives was brought by you.

If there are casualties of war then remember that when they woke up and got dressed in the morning they did not plan to die this day. Allow them dignity in death. Bury them properly and mark their graves.

It is my foremost intention to bring every single one of you out alive. But there may be people among us who will not see the end of this campaign. We will put them in their sleeping bags and send them back. There will be no time for sorrow.

The enemy should be in no doubt that we are his nemesis and that we are bringing about his rightful destruction. There are many regional commanders who have stains on their souls and they are stoking the fires of Hell for Saddam ... As they die they will know their deeds have brought them to this place. Show them no pity.

It is a big step to take another human life. It is not to be done lightly. I know of men who have taken life needlessly in other conflicts. I can assure you they live with the mark of Cain upon them.

If someone surrenders to you then remember they have that right in international law and ensure that one day they go home to their family. The ones who wish to fight, well, we aim to please.

[...]

As for ourselves, let's bring everyone home and leave Iraq a better place for us having been there.

Our business now is North.

——THE CONSEQUENCES——

Collins's speech – with its mix of high rhetoric and locker room colloquialism – was the perfect mission statement for the British in Iraq. His men faced a ruthless enemy, inhospitable terrain, and the threat of WMDs. Collins was there to provide clarity and a sense of purpose that would see them safely through the trials ahead.

Collins's address seems to have worked. His battalion, the First Royal Irish, captured more territory, he later claimed, than any other formation, while suffering no deaths or serious injuries.

But his words, recorded by a British journalist, would reach far beyond the plains of Iraq. In London, the Prince of Wales wrote that the speech encapsulated 'everything we have come to expect of our armed forces'. In America,

President Bush is said to have mounted a framed copy of the transcript on the wall of the Oval Office.

Five years later, Collins's speech was the subject of a BBC drama, delivered by no less an actor than Kenneth Branagh. At a time of deep public disquiet, the speech had reassured people back home that perhaps the invasion of Iraq might be a just war – if not by design, then at least in its execution.

Other Notable Lines

During the 2003 Iraq War, Saddam's Information Minister, Muhammed Saeed al-Sahhaf, became famous for what might be called 'optimistic' pronouncements on his government's war effort. The Baghdad press corps unkindly named him 'Comical Ali'. His statements, as Coalition forces advanced, included such gems as: 'We will push those crooks, those mercenaries back into the swamp'; 'Our initial assessment is that they will all die'; 'They have started to commit suicide under the walls of Baghdad. We will encourage them to commit more suicides quickly.'

Even at the last, with American tanks clearly visible in the streets behind him, al-Sahhaf remained defiant: 'There is no presence of American infidels in the city of Baghdad … We besieged them and we killed most of them. Today the tide has turned.'

Other Notable Lines

In June 1924, the British mountaineer George Mallory was seen climbing up the steep rocks of the North Ridge of Mount Everest. He never returned. It was only seventy-five years later that a team of climbers finally found his broken body, frozen and bleached by years of sun and snow.

Whether Mallory made it to Everest's top is one of mountaineering's great unknowns. If he did, he was the first to do so, beating the next successful expedition by nearly three decades.

But even if Mallory failed, he left one lasting legacy – a casual reply to a reporter's question that became a sort of creed for mountaineers. 'Why do you want to climb Mount Everest?' the reporter asked. Mallory answered: 'Because it's there.'

2008
VICTORY SPEECH

BARACK OBAMA
(1961–)

Barack Obama was an unlikely candidate for the presidency, and even for the Democratic presidential nomination. He was widely considered too young or too inexperienced to hold the highest office – when he announced that he would run, in 2007, he was only in his mid-forties, and had served a mere two years in the federal government.

And then there was his race. Born in Hawaii, to a Kenyan father and a white mother from Kansas, Obama was campaigning to become the first ever African-American president of the United States.

It quickly became clear, however, that he was blessed with an unusual talent for political oratory. In 2004, as a relative unknown, he delivered a keynote speech at the Democratic Convention that catapulted him into the limelight. It had taken him months to prepare – he used to sneak off in the middle of Senate sessions to jot down thoughts – but the effort paid off handsomely. His moving address on the subject of national unity had delegates chanting his name. Out of nowhere, he had become a plausible challenger for the Democratic presidential nomination.

Four years, and several stirring speeches, later, Barack Obama won the presidential election, making history in the process. Addressing a crowd of thousands in Chicago's Grant Park, the soon-to-be-president made his victory speech.

—— THE SPEECH ——

If there is anyone out there who still doubts that America is a place where all things are possible; who still wonders if the dream of our founders is alive in our time; who still questions the power of our democracy, tonight is your answer.

It's the answer told by lines that stretched around schools and churches in numbers this nation has never seen; by people who waited three hours and four hours, many for the very first time in their lives, because they believed that this time must be different; that their voice could be that difference.

It's the answer spoken by young and old, rich and poor, Democrat and Republican, black, white, Latino,

Asian, Native American, gay, straight, disabled and not disabled – Americans who sent a message to the world that we have never been a collection of Red States and Blue States: we are, and always will be, the United States of America.

It's the answer that led those who have been told for so long by so many to be cynical, and fearful, and doubtful of what we can achieve to put their hands on the arc of history and bend it once more toward the hope of a better day.

It's been a long time coming, but tonight, because of what we did on this day, in this election, at this defining moment, change has come to America.

[. . .]

The road ahead will be long. Our climb will be steep. We may not get there in one year or even one term, but America – I have never been more hopeful than I am tonight that we will get there. I promise you – we as a people will get there.

There will be setbacks and false starts. There are many who won't agree with every decision or policy I make as President, and we know that government can't solve every problem. But I will always be honest with you about the challenges we face. I will listen to you, especially when we disagree. And above all, I will ask you join in the work of remaking this nation the only way it's been done in America for two-hundred and twenty-one years – block by block, brick by brick, calloused hand by calloused hand.

What began twenty-one months ago in the depths of winter must not end on this autumn night. This victory alone is not the change we seek – it is only the chance for us to make that change. And that cannot happen if we go back to the way things were. It cannot happen without you.

[. . .]

And to all those watching tonight from beyond our shores, from parliaments and palaces to those who are huddled around radios in the forgotten corners of our world – our stories are singular, but our destiny is shared, and a new dawn of American leadership is at hand. To those who would tear this world down – we will defeat you. To those who seek peace and security – we support you. And to all those who have wondered if America's beacon still burns as bright – tonight we proved once more that the true strength of our nation comes not from the might of our arms or the scale of our wealth, but from the enduring power of our ideals: democracy, liberty, opportunity, and unyielding hope.

For that is the true genius of America – that America can change. Our union can be perfected. And what we have already achieved gives us hope for what we can and must achieve tomorrow.

[. . .]

This is our chance to answer that call. This is our moment. This is our time – to put our people back to work and open doors of opportunity for our kids; to restore prosperity and promote the cause of peace; to reclaim the American Dream and reaffirm that fundamental truth – that out of many, we are one; that while we breathe, we hope, and where we are met with cynicism, and doubt, and those who tell us that we can't, we will respond with that timeless creed that sums up the spirit of a people: Yes We Can.

Thank you, God bless you, and may God bless the United States of America.

—— THE CONSEQUENCES ——

For many who watched that day, Obama, with his message of hope and change, looked more like a saviour than a politician. In a subsequent poll, more Americans nominated Obama as their 'personal hero' than anyone else, including Jesus, Abraham Lincoln and Mother Teresa.

He was modern, youthful, international. Pundits seized on Obama's Kenyan ancestry and Indonesian upbringing to cast him as a citizen of the world – someone who would end destructive US unilateralism. In 2009, the new President was awarded the Nobel Peace Prize, having been in office for less than a year.

To his critics, the Nobel award was a triumph of style over substance. They conceded that Obama was a fine speaker, but at that point, what had he actually done? The Middle Eastern wars remained deadlocked – the outlook gloomy. The economy was floundering. What legislation Obama had pushed through Congress was either dangerously progressive (from a right-wing perspective) or tainted by compromise (looked at from the left).

But Obama had shown that he had new ideas, and that when he needed to, he could be expert at communicating them. It is too soon to say what the ultimate impact of his presidency may be, but armed with such formidable rhetorical skill he and his speeches really could one day change history.

— SOURCES —

John Ball: www.nationalarchives.gov.uk/humanrights/

Napoleon Bonaparte: http://www.gutenberg.org/cache/epub/3563/pg3563.txt

President George W. Bush:
http://www.americanrhetoric.com/speeches/stateoftheunion2002.htm

Winston Churchill: http://bit.ly/gyYByW; http://bit.ly/eJiYsz ; http://bit.ly/9kehYn

Cicero:
http://www.perseus.tufts.edu/hopper/text?doc=Perseus:text:1999.02.0021:speech%3D13

Colonel Tim Collins: http://www.telegraph.co.uk/comment/3562917/Colonel-Tim-Collins-Iraq-war-speech-in-full.html

Oliver Cromwell:
http://www.emersonkent.com/speeches/dismissal_of_the_rump_parliament.htm

Demosthenes:
http://www.perseus.tufts.edu/hopper/text?doc=Perseus:text:1999.01.0070:speech=9

Elizabeth I: http://www.bbc.co.uk/radio4/history/elizabethan_echoes/quotes.shtml

Mohandas Gandhi: http://www.mkgandhi.org/speeches/bhu.htm

Giuseppe Garibaldi: http://www.emersonkent.com/history_notes/giuseppe_garibaldi.htm#I_offer_hunger,_thirst,_forced_marches,_battles,_and_death

Charles de Gaulle: http://www.guardian.co.uk/theguardian/2007/apr/29/greatspeeches1

Adolf Hitler: http://bit.ly/hDVDwa

Homer: http://www.perseus.tufts.edu/hopper/text?doc=Perseus:text:1999.01.0217:book%3D1:card%3D240

Jesus: http://www.kingjamesbibleonline.org/

Chief Joseph: http://www.nezperce.com/npedu11.html

President John F. Kennedy:
http://www.jfklibrary.org/AssetViewer/BqXIEM9F4024ntFl7SVAjA.aspx

Martin Luther King:
http://www.americanrhetoric.com/speeches/mlkihaveadream.htm

Osama bin Laden: http://news.bbc.co.uk/1/hi/world/south_asia/1585636.stm

President Abraham Lincoln:
http://www.americanrhetoric.com/speeches/gettysburgaddress.htm

Harold Macmillan: http://www.famous-speeches-and-speech-topics.info/famous-speeches/harold-macmillan-speech-wind-of-change.htm

Malcolm X: http://www.historytimes.com/fresh-perspectives-in-history/black-history/famous-african-americans/329--the-ballot-or-the-bullet-speech-malcolm-x

Nelson Mandela: http://bit.ly/g2kC9f

Jawaharlal Nehru: http://www.guardian.co.uk/theguardian/2007/may/01/greatspeeches

Barack Obama: http://bit.ly/gvWjLh

Emmeline Pankhurst:
http://www.guardian.co.uk/theguardian/2007/apr/27/greatspeeches1?INTCMP=ILCNETT
XT3487

General George S. Patton: http://www.5ad.org/Patton_speech.htm

Patrick Pearse:
http://www.emersonkent.com/speeches/ireland_unfree_shall_never_be_at_peace.htm

I HAVE A DREAM

Pericles:
http://www.perseus.tufts.edu/hopper/text?doc=Perseus:text:1999.04.0105:book%3D2
President Ronald Reagan: http://www.reaganfoundation.org/pdf/Remarks_on_East_
West_Relations_at_Brandenburg%20Gate_061287.pdf
Maximilien Robespierre:
http://www.historywiz.org/primarysources/justificationterror.htm
Franklin Delano Roosevelt: http://bit.ly/d7j9DR
William Shakespeare: http://www.chronique.com/Library/Knights/crispen.htm
Joseph Stalin: http://www.ibiblio.org/pha/timeline/411107awp.html
Aung San Suu Kyi:
http://www.thirdworldtraveler.com/Burma/FreedomFromFearSpeech.html
Margaret Thatcher: http://www.margaretthatcher.org/document/104431
Sojourner Truth: http://historymatters.gmu.edu/d/5740/
Pope Urban II: http://www.fordham.edu/halsall/source/urban2-5vers.html
Mao Zedong: http://www.marxists.org/reference/archive/mao/works/red-
book/ch05.htm

—— ACKNOWLEDGEMENTS ——

The author and publishers are grateful to the following for permissions to use
material that is in copyright:

Winston Churchill: Reproduced with permission of Curtis Brown Ltd, London
on behalf of the Estate of Sir Winston Churchill: Copyright © Winston S. Churchill.

Colonel Tim Collins: Copyright © Tim Collins 2003.

Martin Luther King: Reprinted by arrangement with The Heirs to the Estate of
Martin Luther King Jr, c/o Writers House as agent for the proprietor New York,
NY. Copyright 1963 Dr Martin Luther King Jr; copyright renewed 1991 Coretta
Scott King.

Nelson Mandela: Extracts reproduced with permission from the
Nelson Mandela Foundation.

George S. Patton: From the collection of Charles M. Province,
The George S. Patton, Jr. Historical Society, www.pattonhq.com.

Margaret Thatcher: Extracts reproduced with permission from
www.margaretthatcher.org, the website of the Margaret Thatcher Foundation
where the full text can be found.